SIX
Ingredients
or Less®
Pasta & Casseroles

Also by Carlean Johnson

Six Ingredients or Less Cookbook
Six Ingredients or Less Chicken Cookbook
Six Ingredients or Less Light and Healthy

SIX
Ingredients
or Less®
Pasta & Casseroles

Carlean Johnson

CJ
BOOKS
Washington

SIX INGREDIENTS OR LESS® PASTA & CASSEROLES

Copyright© 1996 by Carlean Johnson
Seventh printing 2001
Printed in the United States of America

Notice: The information in this book is true to the best of our knowledge, but it is not meant to take the place of skilled professionals and the advice of your doctor. Author and publisher disclaim all liability in connection with the use of this book.

Cover Design by Judy Petry
Cover photo by Fred Milkie
Illustrations by Judy Perkins
Nutritional Analysis by Linda Hazen
Typography and production design by Bev Binkley

Library of Congress Catalog Card Number: 95-70161
ISBN: 0-942878-04-3

C J Books
P O Box 922
Gig Harbor, WA 98335
1-800-423-7184

DEDICATION

This book is dedicated to my son-in-law, Joe Hazen, who has been involved with my books almost from the beginning. He has helped me in numerous ways and always without a word of complaint. Thanks, Joe, for all your help and for being such a wonderful son-in-law.

ACKNOWLEDGMENTS

An author is always given credit for writing a book, but there are always so many others who should be recognized for the tremendous amount of work they do.

First of all, I would like to thank my children Steve, Linda, Brian and Mike, and my grandchildren Laura, Peter, Ashley, Paulina, Mark and Ben for their loyal support. They are my best fans. I once attended a lecture given by a local author who mentioned the lack of support she receives from her children. Even though she is quite famous, her children do not give her the recognition she deserves, nor do they believe she is that well-known. She is just "Mom" to them. After almost 14 years of publishing my cookbooks, my children are just as dedicated and supportive as they were in the beginning. I think most everyone would agree I am a very lucky Mother.

As with my other books, I want to thank my daughter, Linda, for helping me in so many ways and in the long hours she spent doing the nutritional analysis. I know with two small children, it wasn't easy.

I appreciate and want to thank Bev Binkley for all the many long hours she spent in typesetting and designing the text. This was her first book and she did a wonderful job along with her other duties as well.

Another big thank you to Judy Petry for the cover design. Judy is such a good designer and so dedicated to what she does that I feel very lucky to have her on board again for our fourth cover. Judy enjoys working with photographer Fred Milkie and he, once again, came through for us. Fred is so talented and so relaxed, he is a pleasure to work with. Thanks, Fred, for another job well done.

A new member of our team is Judy Perkins from Bernie, MO. Judy and I went to school together and over the years, I have admired her artistic talent and home decorating. Thanks, Judy, for the beautiful illustrations throughout the book.

I also want to thank my neighbor, Lisa Helling, for doing the final proofreading. This is not an easy job and I appreciate the weekend hours she spent doing this for us.

Last, but not least, my granddaughter, Paulina, deserves some credit for getting this book finished on time. She loves to cook and was constantly saying "Let's cook, Grandma. We can do pasta!" Thanks, Paulina, for keeping me on my toes and in the kitchen.

TABLE OF CONTENTS

INTRODUCTION

Instead of pass the potatoes, we now hear pass the pasta! Italian restaurants are very popular right now and most of us have caught on to how good pasta is with its almost endless variety of popular dishes. Pasta is easy to prepare, can be on the table usually within 30 minutes and is absolutely delicious. Almost anything, chicken, meats, vegetables, cheese, leftovers, can be turned into a simple or elegant quick pasta meal. Pasta is unquestionably here to stay.

I have always enjoyed pasta, but after testing an endless number of recipes for this cookbook, I have become absolutely addicted to it. My turning point was when I started using freshly grated, real Parmesan cheese stamped "Parmigiano-Reggiano" on the rind. What a difference in flavor! You'll never want to go back to using anything else. Parmigiano-Reggiano is an Italian grating cheese and is quite expensive, but if you shop around, it may not cost you any more, or perhaps even as much, as the Parmesan cheese most of us are accustomed to purchasing in our local supermarkets.

Even though most pasta dishes, as a rule, are quite easy to prepare, pasta does have its quirks. I am constantly amazed at how quickly pasta dishes cool off. They must be hot to be enjoyed. Serving in heated bowls and plates will help and don't let your guests linger before coming to the table. I also found an accurate weight scale is a must, especially for weighing pasta and cheese. A peppermill is also a must-have, so put these two items on your wish list.

Sauces must adequately coat the pasta for a more pleasing dish and some brands of pasta seem to work better than others, although most brands I purchased were very good. If you have difficulty getting a nice, smooth pasta dish, try tossing with a little bit of the cooking water, or toss the pasta with a small amount of butter before adding the sauce. Sometimes it also helps to reduce the amount of cheese called for in the recipe.

Who isn't familiar with casseroles. We may not always have fond childhood memories of things thrown together and called "dinner", but then again, maybe we didn't have the pleasure of being served premium casseroles with quality ingredients. A good casserole can turn a simple meal into a delicious, no-fuss dinner.

With these recipes, you'll appreciate the convenience and the variety of one-dish meals prepared quickly. Whether you're cooking for your family or entertaining a crowd, casseroles are the perfect way to minimize time spent in the kitchen.

The pleasures of pasta and casseroles are numerous - so Happy Cooking!

NUTRITIONAL ANALYSIS

- Recipe analysis is based on the smallest number of servings or a unit such as one cup, 1 tablespoon, etc.

- The first ingredient is used when more than one is listed.

- When listed as salt and pepper, to taste, amounts are not included since this is left up to individual tastes.

- The analysis can vary somewhat if not measured or weighed accurately.

- When a recipes calls for "milk", 2% milk was used unless otherwise specified.

- Recipe analysis can vary according to brand products used in the recipes.

- A few of the recipes do not have a "Lighter Version". Either it was already low in fat and small changes wouldn't have made that much difference or the recipe could not be converted to lowfat without totally changing the taste and makeup of the recipe (in which case you probably wouldn't enjoy it).

- Some of the recipes have been reduced in fat without losing any of the original flavor. Others may have a slight difference in taste, but hardly noticeable unless you are looking for it. A few recipes may have changed enough that it is up to individual preference as to which version you would rather use.

- I would suggest using quality lowfat ingredients. Try various products as there is often quite a difference among brands. For instance, some lowfat cheeses cannot be detected in cooked dishes, others aren't worth eating no matter what you do with them.

Experiment and Enjoy!

HELPFUL HINTS

1. One of the most important cooking tips I can give you is, "Always read through a recipe before you start". You don't want any last-minute surprises.

2. Most of the recipes are for 4 to 6 servings which can have different meanings according to the number of people being served and the size of their appetites.

3. Salt and pepper is often left up to individual tastes or requirements.

4. In most recipes, it is important to use the size pan or baking dish called for in the recipe. For that reason, a minimum number of cooking dish sizes are called for.

5. Obviously, with just six ingredients or less, not everything is always cooked from scratch, although for those who wish to, there are numerous recipes to choose from.

6. Ingredients don't have to be expensive, but they should be good quality and fresh.

ABOUT THE AUTHOR

Carlean Johnson resides in scenic Gig Harbor, which is located in the Puget Sound area of Washington State. With the success of her first Six Ingredients or Less cookbook, the title became a series, with Pasta and Casseroles being her fourth book. Satisfied customers are already asking about the next book in the series.

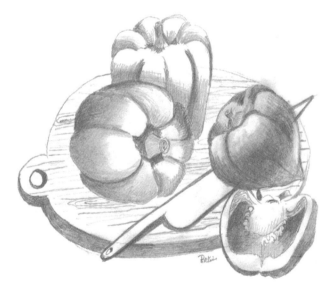

Pasta

Won Ton Noodle Appetizer

*An irresistible appetizer or first course. Have some ready in the freezer
the next time you want to entertain.*

1 (12-ounce) package sausage
1 (14-ounce) package won ton wrappers
1/2 cup thinly sliced green onions (about 3 onions)
11/2 cups (6-ounces) Monterey Jack cheese with jalapeno, shredded
3 cups vegetable oil
Salsa or spaghetti sauce (optional)

Crumble sausage in skillet and cook over medium heat. When sausage has
partially cooked, mash the meat with the back of a fork to make smaller
pieces. Continue cooking until cooked through; drain thoroughly.

Fill center of each won ton with about 1 teaspoon sausage. Top with 3 or 4
slices green onion and a small amount of cheese. Moisten edges of wrapper
with water. Fold over diagonally to form a triangle and press edges firmly
with a fork to seal. Then moisten the two ends of the triangle and bring
ends together overlapping about an inch; press tightly to seal. These will
resemble a large tortellini.

Heat oil in a deep saucepan and cook won tons a few at a time. They will
quickly rise to the top and brown. Turn and brown other side. Remove and
drain on paper towels. Serve immediately as a finger food or place 3 won
tons in center of a small serving plate with points directed out. Garnish
center with large sprig of parsley. Serve with salsa or spaghetti sauce, if
desired. Makes 48.

Lighter Version
Light turkey sausage
Salsa

Per pc.	Cal	Pro	Carb	Fib	Fat	Sat	Chol	Sod
Regular	62	2g	5g	0g	3g	1g	7mg	113mg
Lighter	58	3g	5g	0g	3g	0g	8mg	116mg

Toasted Ravioli

This is a delicious appetizer or snack recipe, but must be cooked just before serving. Amount of each ingredient will be determined by how many you wish to serve.

Top Of Stove

Vegetable oil
Fresh ravioli - try different fillings to find your favorite
Milk
Dry Italian bread crumbs
Freshly grated Parmesan cheese
Salsa, pizza sauce or seasoned tomato sauce

Heat oil in large saucepan (you will need at least 2 to 3 inches). Place milk and bread crumbs in small bowls. Dip ravioli in milk, then in bread crumbs. Carefully drop, a few at a time, into hot oil; turn to brown other side. Cooking time is very short; ravioli should rise to the top of the oil, puff up in the center and be nicely toasted on both sides. Drain on paper towels. Immediately sprinkle with grated Parmesan cheese. Serve with sauce.

TIP: Oil should be hot enough for deep-frying in order for the ravioli to puff up nicely in center. These do not reheat well.

Lemon Cream with Ravioli

This rich pasta is accented with a delicious light lemon sauce.

2 cups whipping cream
1 lemon
2 tablespoons freshly ground black pepper
2 tablespoons coarsely chopped parsley
1 (9-ounce) package fresh ravioli (your choice of filling)
2 tablespoons freshly grated Parmesan cheese

Pour cream into a medium skillet. Bring to a boil and reduce heat to simmer. Grate lemon peel and add half the peel to the cream (save remaining peel for garnish). Squeeze juice from lemon and add 3 tablespoons to the cream. Continue cooking sauce until reduced to half (about 1 cup). This will take about 10 to 12 minutes. Meanwhile, cook ravioli according to package directions; drain. Add ground pepper and parsley to cream mixture. Add pasta and gently toss to coat. Sprinkle with Parmesan cheese. Makes 4 appetizer or first-course servings or 2 main-dish servings.

TIP: If a milder lemon flavor is desired, use 2 tablespoons juice. To time the pasta and cream to be ready at the same time, I would suggest bringing the water to a boil and adding the pasta about 5 or 6 minutes before sauce is ready.

Lighter Version:
Half and Half

	Cal	Pro	Carb	Fib	Fat	Sat	Chol	Sod
Regular	686	13g	57g	4g	46g	28g	165mg	107mg
Lighter	426	13g	59g	4g	16g	9g	46mg	83mg

Ravioli with Butter Sauce

Impress your friends with this easy and attractive pasta dish.

1 (9-ounce) package fresh cheese-filled ravioli
1/3 cup butter
1 medium garlic clove, minced
2 tablespoons pine nuts
Coarsely chopped parsley (for garnish)

Cook ravioli according to package directions; drain. Meanwhile, melt butter in small skillet. Add garlic and pine nuts. Cook over low heat until pine nuts are lightly browned (watch carefully - this doesn't take long). Place about 10 ravioli on each serving plate. Top with some of the butter sauce. Sprinkle with parsley. Makes 4 appetizer or first-course servings or 2 main-dish servings.

	Cal	Pro	Carb	Fib	Fat	Sat	Chol	Sod
Regular	360	11g	23g	0g	26g	12g	97mg	343mg
Lighter	327	11g	23g	0g	22g	10g	87mg	305mg

Walnut Basil Fettuccine

Rich enough for a main meal. Add your favorite salad, bread and dessert.

12 ounces fettuccine
$1/4$ cup olive oil
3 large garlic cloves, minced
$3/4$ cup coarsely chopped walnuts
$1/4$ cup chopped fresh basil
$2/3$ cup freshly grated Parmesan cheese

Cook pasta according to package directions; drain and return to pot. Meanwhile, during last 6 to 7 minutes pasta is cooking, heat olive oil in medium nonstick skillet. Add garlic and walnuts. Cook over medium heat, stirring frequently, until walnuts are lightly toasted. Remove from heat; stir in basil.

Add Parmesan cheese to pasta and toss to coat. Add walnut mixture. Serve immediately. Makes 4 side-dish servings or 2 main-dish servings.

TIP: The garlic is less likely to stick to the pan if you use a nonstick skillet. Also, it would be wise to save just a little bit of the hot pasta water just in case too much of the oil is cooked away. You may need to add additional liquid to make a smooth coating for the pasta.

<u>Lighter Version:</u>
$1/3$ cup walnuts
$1/2$ cup Parmesan cheese

	Cal	Pro	Carb	Fib	Fat	Sat	Chol	Sod
Regular	674	24g	71g	5g	33g	6g	13mg	310mg
Lighter	576	19g	70g	4g	25g	5g	10mg	236mg

Vermicelli with Mascarpone

This recipe lends itself to convenient "on hand" ingredients that can be thrown together for a quick, yet delectable, meal.

Top Of Stove

1 pound vermicelli
1 (8-ounce) container Mascarpone cheese, room temperature
1/4 cup chopped fresh parsley
1/2 cup freshly grated Parmesan cheese

Cook pasta according to package directions; drain. Toss pasta with the Mascarpone cheese and parsley in a large heated bowl. Place on individual serving plates and sprinkle with the Parmesan cheese. Makes 4 main-dish servings.

TIP: This pasta dish tends to cool off very rapidly, but does reheat nicely in a microwave oven. Place on individual servings plates, reheat in microwave, then sprinkle with Parmesan cheese.

VARIATION: Add cooked chicken and peas, salmon and fresh dill, tuna and capers, pork or beef strips.

	Cal	Pro	Carb	Fib	Fat	Sat	Chol	Sod
Regular	758	23g	92g	5g	32g	3g	88mg	272mg

Swiss Noodles with Pecans

This is one of those pasta dishes that looks like you put a lot of effort into it. Serve on one of your most attractive serving dishes.

Top of Stove

12 ounces fettuccine
6 tablespoons butter, melted
2 cups (8-ounces) Swiss cheese, shredded
Ground black pepper to taste
1 tablespoon finely chopped pecans
1 tablespoon chopped parsley

Cook pasta according to package directions; drain well and return to pot. Add melted butter and gradually stir in the cheese. Add ground pepper to taste. Place on serving platter. Sprinkle with pecans, then parsley. Makes 4 servings.

TIP: If you forget to add the ground pepper, as I sometimes have, don't worry - I doubt you will miss it.

Lighter Version:
2 tablespoons butter
Lowfat Swiss cheese

	Cal	Pro	Carb	Fib	Fat	Sat	Chol	Sod
Regular	711	28g	69g	4g	36g	21g	99mg	326mg
Lighter	498	28g	69g	4g	11g	6g	35mg	209mg

Spinach Tortellini with Pecan Sauce

A sinfully delicious pasta dish with a very rich sauce. This one receives raves every time.

Top Of Stove

1 (9-ounce) package fresh spinach tortellini with cheese filling
2 tablespoons olive oil
$1/2$ cup chopped pecans
1 cup whipping cream
1 cup, plus 2 tablespoons, freshly grated Parmesan cheese
Freshly ground black pepper

Cook pasta according to package directions; drain. Meanwhile, heat olive oil in a small deep skillet or saucepan. Add pecans and lightly toast over medium heat (watch carefully; after a certain point, they burn easily).

Add cream and bring to a boil. Turn off heat; gradually add the 1 cup Parmesan cheese, stirring until melted and smooth. Place noodles on a medium serving plate with a slight rim; pour sauce over top. Sprinkle with ground pepper and remaining Parmesan cheese. Makes 4 side-dish servings or 2 main-dish servings.

Lighter Version:
$1/4$ cup pecans
Canned evaporated skim milk
$1/2$ cup Parmesan cheese

	Cal	Pro	Carb	Fib	Fat	Sat	Chol	Sod
Regular	695	24g	36g	1g	52g	23g	130mg	726mg
Lighter	355	18g	36g	0g	16g	6g	41mg	443mg

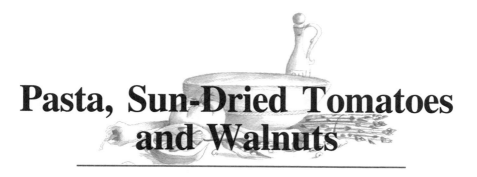

Pasta, Sun-Dried Tomatoes and Walnuts

The sun-dried tomatoes lends a slight tart flavor to this delicious pasta dish. Excellent served with Chicken Parmesan and most fish entrees.

Top Of Stove

10 ounces mostoccioli or penne
$1/4$ cup chopped oil-packed, sun-dried tomatoes plus 3 tablespoons of the oil
$1/2$ cup sliced green onions (white and green part)
$1/3$ cup coarsely chopped walnuts
$1/2$ cup whipping cream
$2/3$ cup freshly grated Parmesan cheese, divided

Cook pasta according to package directions; drain. Meanwhile, heat oil from the tomatoes in a large deep skillet. Add onions and walnuts. Cook until onions are soft; add sun-dried tomatoes and cream and heat through. Add pasta and toss to coat. Sprinkle with $1/3$ cup of the Parmesan cheese and toss to melt. Pour onto a large platter or deep bowl. Sprinkle with remaining Parmesan cheese. Makes 6 side-dish servings.

TIP: This recipe reheats better than most pasta dishes.

Lighter Version:
Reduce oil to 1 tablespoon
Canned evaporated skim milk
Omit Parmesan cheese on top

	Cal	Pro	Carb	Fib	Fat	Sat	Chol	Sod
Regular	428	14g	42g	3g	23g	8g	36mg	240mg
Lighter	286	10g	43g	3g	8g	1g	1mg	52mg

Parsley Butter Pasta Dish

A smooth and light-flavored pasta dish that goes with most meat and chicken dishes.

Top Of Stove

8 ounces linguine
6 tablespoons butter, melted
¹/₄ cup chopped fresh parsley
¹/₃ cup freshly grated Parmesan cheese

Cook pasta according to package directions; drain and place in large serving bowl. Add butter and parsley; toss to coat. Stir in Parmesan until melted and smooth. Makes 4 servings.

<u>Lighter Version:</u>
2 tablespoons butter

	Cal	Pro	Carb	Fib	Fat	Sat	Chol	Sod
Regular	413	11g	45g	3g	21g	13g	53mg	333mg
Lighter	312	11g	45g	3g	9g	5g	22mg	216mg

Linguine with Lemon

A smooth sauce with a wonderful light lemon flavor.

Top Of Stove

8 ounces linguine
2 tablespoons olive oil
1 large garlic clove, minced
1/2 cup whipping cream
3 tablespoons fresh lemon juice (or to taste)
1/2 cup freshly grated Parmesan cheese

Cook pasta according to package directions; drain. Meanwhile, heat oil in large skillet. Saute garlic for about 1 minute. Stir in cream and lemon juice; heat until warm. Add pasta and toss to mix. Add Parmesan cheese and toss. Let stand a few minutes to absorb some of the sauce. Makes 6 side-dish servings.

<u>Lighter Version:</u>
Reduce oil to 1 tablespoon
Canned evaporated skim milk
1/4 cup Parmesan cheese

	Cal	Pro	Carb	Fib	Fat	Sat	Chol	Sod
Regular	297	9g	31g	2g	15g	7g	34mg	164mg
Lighter	206	8g	33g	2g	4g	1g	4mg	103mg

Easy Fettuccine Alfredo

It would be hard to find an easier sauce than this one.

Top Of Stove

16 ounces fettuccine
1/2 cup butter, softened
3/4 cup freshly grated Parmesan cheese
1/4 cup whipping cream
Freshly ground black pepper, to taste

Cook pasta according to package directions; drain. In small mixer bowl, lightly beat butter; add Parmesan cheese and mix thoroughly. Add cream and blend. Toss mixture with hot pasta and ground pepper. Makes 4 main-dish servings and 8 side-dish servings.

Enjoy!

	Cal	Pro	Carb	Fib	Fat	Sat	Chol	Sod
Regular	784	23g	90g	5g	36g	22g	97mg	592mg

Creamy Cheese and Noodles

An Alfredo type sauce so quick and easy you can have dinner on the table in minutes. This recipe can be used as a side dish or double the recipe, add some cooked chicken or shrimp, and serve as a main dish for four.

Top Of Stove

8 ounces dumplings (see TIP)
2 tablespoons butter
1/2 cup whipping cream
1/4 cup freshly grated Parmesan Cheese

Cook dumplings according to package directions; drain and return to pan. Meanwhile, heat butter and cream until butter is melted. Add cream mixture to pasta and toss to coat. Add Parmesan cheese; toss until melted and smooth. Makes 4 side-dish servings.

TIP: Dumplings, at least in my part of the country, are made by Creamette. They are an inch or so long and have ruffled edges. If you can't find Dumplings, or don't have time to shop around, use bowties or shells.

<u>Lighter Version:</u>
1 1/2 tablespoons butter
Canned evaporated skim milk
3 tablespoons Parmesan cheese

	Cal	Pro	Carb	Fib	Fat	Sat	Chol	Sod
Regular	404	11g	46g	2g	20g	12g	61mg	188mg
Lighter	306	12g	48g	2g	7g	4g	16mg	169mg

Browned Butter with Myzithra

My daughter, Linda, introduced me to this quick and easy recipe. It has a nice blend of flavors and is similar to a pasta served at the Spaghetti Factory.

Top Of Stove

8 ounces spaghetti
1/3 cup butter
2 medium garlic cloves, minced
1/2 cup grated Myzithra cheese

Cook pasta according to package directions; drain. In a small skillet, melt butter over medium-low heat. Add garlic and cook until butter turns a light brown. (Watch carefully at this point. If it turns too dark, it will have to be discarded.) Add butter to pasta and toss to coat. Place on individual serving dishes and sprinkle with about 2 tablespoons cheese. Makes 4 side-dish servings or 2 main dishes.

Ben's Broccoli Cheese Pasta

My ten-month old grandson, Ben, thought this was quite a treat. A can of soup and some pasta and you have a meal - almost. This is an excellent quick family dish that requires just a few ingredients.

Top Of Stove

8 ounces thin spaghetti
1 tablespoon butter
1/4 cup finely chopped onion
1 can Broccoli Cheese soup
1/2 cup milk
3 tablespoons freshly grated Parmesan cheese

Cook pasta according to package directions; drain and return to pot. Meanwhile, melt butter in small saucepan. Add onion and saute until soft. Add soup; stir in milk until blended. Cook over low heat until heated through. Pour over pasta; toss to mix. Place on serving platter and sprinkle with Parmesan cheese. Makes 4 servings.

VARIATION: For a more filling main dish, add 1 1/2 cups cubed cooked chicken.

Lighter Version:
Substitute 1 teaspoon olive oil for the butter
Nonfat milk
4 teaspoons Parmesan cheese

	Cal	Pro	Carb	Fib	Fat	Sat	Chol	Sod
Regular	352	13g	53g	4g	10g	5g	18mg	672mg
Lighter	324	11g	53g	4g	7g	3g	8mg	594mg

Fettuccine with Broccoli

Another beautiful pasta dish that can be made in less than 30 minutes.
Serve with a hearty tossed salad, toasted French bread and a yummy
dessert.

Top of Stove

10 ounces fettuccine
3 cups broccoli flowerets
3 tablespoons butter
2 cups whipping cream
1 cup freshly grated Parmesan cheese

Cook fettuccine according to package directions; drain and return to pot. Cook broccoli in butter until just crisp-tender. Add cream and bring to a boil. Add to pasta in pot and heat slightly. Remove from heat and stir in Parmesan cheese; mix lightly but thoroughly. Makes 6 servings.

TIP: Timing is important in this recipe. The one thing you don't want to do is overcook the broccoli -- it should be just crisp-tender when heated with the cream. This mixture should not be allowed to stand while waiting for the fettuccine to cook. (Likewise, the fettuccine shouldn't be allowed to stand after cooking unless it is rinsed with cold water or tossed with a little butter or oil.) Isn't cooking fun!!

Lighter Version:
Omit butter and steam broccoli
Half and Half

	Cal	Pro	Carb	Fib	Fat	Sat	Chol	Sod
Regular	896	24g	64g	5g	62g	38g	206mg	618mg
Lighter	567	25g	65g	5g	23g	14g	64mg	534mg

Pasta Primavera

A quick version of a classic recipe.

8 ounces rigatoni
1 (16-ounce) package frozen mixed cauliflower, carrots and snow peas
$1/2$ cup butter, cubed
1 cup whipping cream
$3/4$ cup freshly grated Parmesan cheese
Pepper

Cook pasta according to package directions; drain and return to pot. Meanwhile, cook vegetables until tender, but not soft. Add butter to pasta and stir to melt. Add whipping cream and Parmesan cheese; toss to coat. Add vegetables and pepper to taste. Cook until heated through. Makes 4 main dish servings.

VARIATION: Use any combination of fresh vegetables:

| Asparagus | Snow Peas | Broccoli | Zucchini |
| Carrots | Cauliflower | Onion | Chopped tomatoes |

Lighter Version:
1 tablespoon butter
Canned evaporated skim milk
$1/3$ cup Parmesan cheese

	Cal	Pro	Carb	Fib	Fat	Sat	Chol	Sod
Regular	781	20g	61g	8g	52g	32g	158mg	646mg
Lighter	399	19g	67g	8g	7g	4g	17mg	296mg

Pasta With Three Peppers

With just a few ingredients, this makes a lot of pasta. Will serve 4 as a main dish or 8 as a vegetable dish.

Top Of Stove

8 ounces fettuccine
2 tablespoons olive oil
2 medium onions, sliced thin (about 4 cups)
3 medium bell peppers (1 red, 1 yellow, 1 green), cut into narrow strips
1 cup whipping cream
1/2 cup freshly grated Parmesan cheese

Cook pasta according to package directions; drain and return to pot. Meanwhile, heat oil in large deep skillet. Separate onion slices into rings and cook over medium heat until onions are just soft. Add pepper strips and cook until crisp-tender, stirring frequently. Add cream and bring to a boil. Toss onion mixture with the pasta. Add Parmesan cheese and toss to melt. Makes 6 servings.

TIP: Do not overcook the onion and peppers. You want a slight crunch to the vegetables.

Lighter Version:
1 tablespoon oil
Canned evaporated skim milk

	Cal	Pro	Carb	Fib	Fat	Sat	Chol	Sod
Regular	627	17g	60g	7g	34g	17g	91mg	263mg
Lighter	442	20g	71g	7g	9g	3g	12mg	314mg

Spaghetti with Onions and Asparagus

This meatless pasta dish is packed with flavor and color.

8 ounces spaghetti
1 tablespoon butter
2/3 cup finely chopped onion
6 ounces fresh asparagus
2/3 cup whipping cream
1/3 cup freshly grated Parmesan cheese

Cook spaghetti according to package directions, drain and return to pot. Meanwhile, heat butter in medium nonstick skillet. Add onion and asparagus and saute 7 to 8 minutes or until onion is soft and asparagus is just crisp tender. While vegetables are cooking, heat whipping cream in a small saucepan and cook gently about 2 minutes. Remove from heat and stir in cheese. Add to vegetable mixture. Pour over pasta and toss to coat. Makes 4 servings.

VARIATION: Add julienned strips of ham or Canadian bacon.

Lighter Version:
Canned evaporated skim milk
1/4 cup Parmesan cheese

	Cal	Pro	Carb	Fib	Fat	Sat	Chol	Sod
Regular	441	13g	50g	4g	21g	13g	68mg	205mg
Lighter	352	14g	53g	4g	9g	5g	25mg	197mg

Zucchini and Mushrooms with Pasta

An attractive recipe that tastes as good as it looks. Serve as a main dish or a vegetable dish.

Top Of Stove

8 ounces fettuccine
6 tablespoons butter, divided
4 ounces fresh mushrooms, sliced
2 medium-small zucchini (about a half pound), cut into julienne strips
1/2 cup whipping cream
1/3 cup freshly grated Parmesan cheese

Cook fettuccine according to package directions; drain and return to pot. Meanwhile, melt 2 tablespoons of the butter in a large skillet. Add mushrooms and cook about 2 minutes, stirring frequently. Add zucchini, cream and remaining 4 tablespoons butter. Bring to a simmer; add Parmesan cheese. Continue to cook, stirring frequently, until sauce is smooth. Pour over pasta; toss briefly to mix. Cover and let stand three or four minutes or until pasta has absorbed most of the sauce. Makes 3 large servings for a lunch or dinner meal or 6 servings as a vegetable.

TIP: Some of the cheese may stick to the bottom of the skillet and can be very difficult to clean. If this happens, fill skillet with enough water to cover cheese. Bring to a boil; remove skillet from burner, carefully pour off hot water and clean immediately.

Lighter Version:
Reduce butter to 3 tablespoons
Canned evaporated skim milk

	Cal	Pro	Carb	Fib	Fat	Sat	Chol	Sod
Regular	1056	26g	97g	7g	64g	39g	188mg	689mg
Lighter	748	29g	103g	7g	25g	14g	62mg	564mg

Baked Mostaccioli and Cream

Occasionally we want a recipe that doesn't need a lot of last minute attention. This is such a recipe. If necessary, it can stand 10 to 15 minutes before serving.

Top Of Stove
Oven 350°

8 ounces mostaccioli
2¹/₂ cups Half and Half, divided
2 tablespoons butter, melted
1 cup (4-ounces) Swiss cheese, shredded
¹/₃ cup freshly grated Parmesan cheese
Nutmeg

Cook pasta according to package directions, cooking about 9 to 10 minutes; drain. Meanwhile, pour 2 cups of the Half and Half in a heavy medium saucepan and heat. While cream is heating, pour melted butter in 8x8-inch baking dish. Sprinkle with half the Swiss cheese.

Add cooked pasta to Half and Half and cook over medium heat about 20 minutes or until liquid is absorbed, stirring frequently. Watch very carefully and stir frequently the last few minutes. Spoon half the pasta into the baking dish. Sprinkle with remaining Swiss cheese. Top with remaining pasta. Add the remaining ¹/₂ cup Half and Half. Top with Parmesan cheese and a light sprinkle of nutmeg. Bake at 350° for 30 minutes or until liquid is absorbed. Makes 6 servings.

Lighter Version:
Omit butter; spray dish with nonstick cooking spray
Lowfat Swiss cheese
3 tablespoons Parmesan cheese

	Cal	Pro	Carb	Fib	Fat	Sat	Chol	Sod
Regular	409	16g	35g	2g	23g	14g	69mg	233mg
Lighter	327	15g	35g	2g	14g	9g	46mg	149mg

Noodle Pudding

This recipe makes an excellent side dish or serve with soup, salad, fruit and rolls.

Top Of Stove
Oven 350°

16 ounces egg noodles
¹/₂ cup butter, cut up
1 cup sugar
10 eggs
³/₄ cup milk
Jam or preserves (optional)

Cook noodles according to package directions, but slightly undercook since they will continue to cook in the oven. Meanwhile, place butter in a large bowl. In another bowl, combine the sugar, eggs and milk. Drain noodles; pour over butter and toss to coat. Add egg mixture and toss gently to coat. Pour into 13x9-inch baking dish sprayed with nonstick cooking spray. Bake at 350° for 35 to 40 minutes or until eggs are set. Cut into squares and, if desired, serve with a small amount of jam or preserves. Makes 12 servings.

VARIATION: Add raisins to mixture before baking. Sprinkle "lightly" with nutmeg.

Lighter Version:
¹/₄ cup butter
Egg substitute
Nonfat milk

	Cal	Pro	Carb	Fib	Fat	Sat	Chol	Sod
Regular	325	10g	41g	1g	13g	7g	229mg	143mg
Lighter	268	11g	41g	1g	7g	3g	42mg	142mg

Pesto Lasagna

*After the fourth try, this turned out to be a keeper. If your family likes
pesto, this should become a favorite.*

Top Of Stove
Oven 350°

8 lasagna noodles
1 egg
1 cup dry curd cottage cheese
1/2 cup pesto sauce
1/2 cup freshly grated Parmesan cheese
12 ounces Mozzarella cheese, shredded, divided

Cook pasta according to package directions; drain and rinse with cold water. Place 4 noodles in a 13x9-inch baking dish sprayed with nonstick cooking spray.

Combine next 4 ingredients in food processor or blender and process until smooth and light. Spread evenly over noodles. Sprinkle with 1 cup (4-ounces) of the Mozzarella cheese. Top with remaining noodles. Sprinkle with remaining cheese making sure all of the noodles are covered. Cover with foil; bake at 350° for 25 to 30 minutes. Remove foil and place under broiler 2 to 3 minutes to lightly brown the cheese. Makes 8 servings.

Lighter Version:
Egg substitute
Light Mozzarella cheese

	Cal	Pro	Carb	Fib	Fat	Sat	Chol	Sod
Regular	327	23g	19g	1g	17g	8g	60mg	457mg
Lighter	275	19g	18g	1g	14g	6g	24mg	348mg

Pasta Frittata with Pesto

This particular recipe reminds me of a good quiche. It can be a brunch, lunch or supper dish and looks wonderful baked in a quiche dish. Because of the dominant pesto flavor, you will want to use your favorite pesto recipe or a good quality store brand.

Top Of Stove
Oven 350°

6 ounces spaghetti
6 eggs, lightly beaten
¹/4 cup pesto
1 cup (4-ounces) Mozzarella cheese, shredded
¹/2 cup freshly grated Parmesan cheese

Cook pasta according to package directions; drain and place in a 10-inch quiche baking dish (or pie dish) sprayed with nonstick cooking spray. Quickly combine eggs and pesto. Add Mozzarella cheese and pour over spaghetti. Sprinkle with Parmesan cheese. Bake at 350° for 20 minutes or until set. Makes 6 servings.

Lighter Version:
Egg substitute
Light Mozzarella cheese
Omit Parmesan cheese

	Cal	Pro	Carb	Fib	Fat	Sat	Chol	Sod
Regular	328	20g	25g	1g	16g	6g	232mg	387mg
Lighter	266	18g	24g	1g	11g	4g	14mg	276mg

Cheesy Macaroni and Cheese

This is an excellent busy day recipe, but you must use a good quality cheese for best results.

Top Of Stove
Oven 350°

1 cup (4-ounces) elbow macaroni
1/2 cup milk
3 cups (12-ounces) medium Cheddar cheese, shredded
Pepper, to taste

Cook macaroni according to package directions; drain and rinse. Meanwhile, heat milk in medium-heavy saucepan. Reduce heat; gradually add cheese, stirring until melted and smooth. Add pepper. Place macaroni in 1 1/2-quart deep casserole dish sprayed with nonstick cooking spray. Pour cheese over macaroni and gently stir to mix. Bake, uncovered, at 350° for 25 to 30 minutes or until heated through and golden. Makes 4 servings.

VARIATION: Top with 3/4 cup buttered bread crumbs for added crunch.

Lighter Version:
Nonfat milk
Lowfat Cheddar cheese

	Cal	Pro	Carb	Fib	Fat	Sat	Chol	Sod
Regular	468	26g	25g	1g	29g	18g	92mg	544mg
Lighter	268	25g	25g	1g	7g	4g	18mg	34mg

Stove Top Macaroni and Cheese

This makes a simple and delicious side dish. Children love it with toasted bread slices and fruit. The whipping cream adds a slight sweet taste and the nutmeg add lots of flavor.

1¹/₂ cups elbow macaroni
1 cup milk
¹/₂ cup whipping cream
2 dashes ground nutmeg (not too much)
3 tablespoons freshly grated Parmesan cheese

Cook macaroni according to package directions. Drain thoroughly and put in medium saucepan. Stir in milk, whipping cream, and nutmeg. Bring to a boil and cook over medium heat about 6 to 8 minutes or until liquid is absorbed. Watch carefully the last couple of minutes to prevent macaroni from sticking to pan; stir frequently. Pour into 8x8-inch baking dish sprayed lightly with nonstick cooking spray. Sprinkle evenly with Parmesan cheese. Place under preheated broiler and broil 2 to 3 minutes or until cheese is golden. Makes 6 servings (more if serving children).

Lighter Version:
Nonfat milk
Half and Half
2 tablespoons Parmesan cheese

	Cal	Pro	Carb	Fib	Fat	Sat	Chol	Sod
Regular	206	7g	23g	1g	10g	6g	33mg	87mg
Lighter	153	6g	24g	1g	3g	2g	10mg	69mg

Butter and Parmesan Cheese with Pasta

A perfect combination of flavors. Serve as a side dish with your choice of meat, poultry or seafood.

Top Of Stove

12 ounces spaghetti
¹/₂ cup butter
¹/₂ cup freshly grated Parmesan cheese
Freshly ground black pepper
Garnish with chopped parsley (optional)

Cook spaghetti according to package directions; drain. Meanwhile, slice butter and place in a large serving bowl. Add pasta and gently toss until butter is melted. Add Parmesan cheese and pepper. Toss until cheese is melted and smooth. Makes 6 side-dish servings.

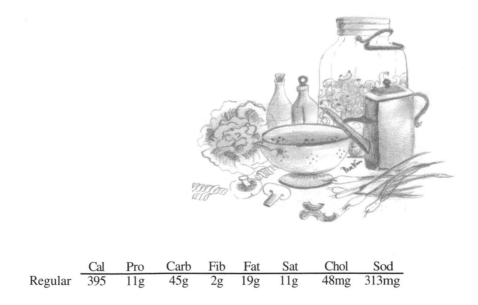

	Cal	Pro	Carb	Fib	Fat	Sat	Chol	Sod
Regular	395	11g	45g	2g	19g	11g	48mg	313mg

Parmesan Noodles

This recipe makes a delicious main dish, but is equally as good as a side dish.

8 ounces spaghetti
3 tablespoons butter
1-2 cloves garlic, minced
$1/3$ cup freshly grated Parmesan cheese
$1/2$ cup heavy cream
Freshly ground pepper

Cook pasta according to package directions; drain. Meanwhile, melt butter in small skillet. Add garlic; saute about 2 minutes. Return drained spaghetti to cooking pot. Stir in butter, Parmesan cheese, cream and ground pepper. Makes 2 medium-size servings as a main dish.

	Cal	Pro	Carb	Fib	Fat	Sat	Chol	Sod
Regular	881	24g	93g	5g	46g	28g	141mg	509mg

Swiss Cheese Pasta

*This recipe can also be made with a variety of cheeses, such
as Fontina, Brie, Jarlsberg, etc.*

Top Of Stove

8 ounces fettuccini
1 cup whipping cream
1 cup (4-ounces) Swiss cheese, shredded
1 tablespoon butter
2 tablespoons chopped parsley
1 tablespoon freshly grated Parmesan cheese

Cook fettuccine according to directions on package. Meanwhile, during
last 3 to 4 minutes of cooking time, bring cream to a boil, remove from heat
and gradually add cheese, stirring until smooth. If the last bit of cheese
doesn't seem to be blending well, return to low heat until smooth. Drain
pasta; toss with butter and parsley. Add cheese sauce and toss gently to
mix. Place on a serving plate and sprinkle with Parmesan cheese. Makes 4
servings.

Lighter Version
Canned evaporated milk
Lowfat Swiss cheese

	Cal	Pro	Carb	Fib	Fat	Sat	Chol	Sod
Regular	562	17g	47g	2g	34g	21g	115mg	154mg
Lighter	399	22g	52g	2g	11g	6g	39mg	214mg

Chicken Mozzarella with Pasta

This easy-to-make chicken dish is great anytime. In this recipe, the pasta is served as a side dish with the chicken.

Top Of Stove

8 ounces pasta (your choice: spaghetti, penne, rotini, etc.)
4 chicken breast halves, skinned and boned
1/4 cup flour
3 tablespoons oil, divided
4 slices (about 4 ounces) Mozzarella cheese
2 cups chunky spaghetti sauce

Cook pasta according to package directions; drain. Meanwhile, place each chicken breast between wax paper and roll or pound with a rolling pin to 1/4-inch thickness; coat with flour. Heat 2 tablespoons oil in a large skillet and cook chicken over medium-high heat 3 to 4 minutes or until lightly browned on one side. Turn and cook about 3 minutes or until cooked through. Top each chicken breast with a slice of Mozzarella cheese, cover skillet and cook about 1 minute or until cheese is soft. Meanwhile, heat spaghetti sauce in a small saucepan. Pour about 1/2 cup sauce on each dinner plate and top with chicken. Toss pasta with remaining oil and place along side the chicken. Makes 4 servings.

TIP: For added color, serve a green vegetable with the dinner or sprinkle a little parsley or basil over the melted cheese.

Lighter Version:
Omit oil
Cook chicken in nonstick skillet sprayed with cooking spray
Light Mozzarella cheese

	Cal	Pro	Carb	Fib	Fat	Sat	Chol	Sod
Regular	626	45g	65g	5g	21g	5g	88mg	872mg
Lighter	566	45g	65g	5g	14g	5g	88mg	872mg

Apricot Chicken with Noodles

This recipe has a light delicate sauce that is perfect teamed with noodles.

4 chicken breast halves, skinned
1/4 cup butter, plus 1 tablespoon, melted
1 tablespoon Dijon mustard
1/2 cup sour cream
1/2 cup apricot preserves
10 ounces egg noodles

Place chicken, skin-side up, in 8x8-inch baking dish. Pour 1/4 cup melted butter over top. Bake in 375° oven for 25 minutes, basting once. Combine mustard, sour cream and apricot preserves; mix well to blend. Remove chicken from oven; pour sauce over top. Bake 25 minutes or until chicken is cooked through. Meanwhile, cook noodles, drain and toss with the 1 tablespoon butter. Place noodles on serving plate and top with chicken. Makes 4 servings.

VARIATION: For a special dinner, garnish with 2 tablespoons sliced, toasted almonds.

Lighter Version:
Reduce butter to 3 tablespoons
Light sour cream
Pasta made without eggs

	Cal	Pro	Carb	Fib	Fat	Sat	Chol	Sod
Regular	616	35g	62g	3g	26g	14g	170mg	346mg
Lighter	582	36g	72g	3g	17g	9g	108mg	276mg

Chicken Cacciatore

This hearty Italian dish can be prepared quickly.

Top Of Stove

8 ounces spaghetti
1 tablespoon olive oil
1 medium garlic clove, minced
4 chicken breast halves, skinned and boned
¼ cup dry white wine
2 cups chunky spaghetti sauce with mushrooms

Cook spaghetti according to package directions; drain. Meanwhile, heat oil in medium skillet. Add garlic and cook about one minute, stirring frequently. Add chicken, rounded side down. Cook, about 3 minutes or until lightly browned. Turn and brown other side. Add wine and spaghetti sauce. Bring sauce to a boil; reduce heat and simmer about 7 to 8 minutes or until chicken is cooked through. Place spaghetti on individual dinner plates; top with chicken. Makes 4 servings.

Lighter Version:
Use 1 teaspoon oil and nonstick skillet

	Cal	Pro	Carb	Fib	Fat	Sat	Chol	Sod
Regular	499	36g	58g	5g	12g	2g	73mg	722mg
Lighter	479	36g	58g	5g	10g	2g	73mg	722mg

Chicken Alfredo

A popular sauce teamed with the ever-popular chicken.

Top Of Stove

8 ounces linguine
4 chicken breast halves, skinned and boned
3 tablespoons plus $^2/_3$ cup freshly grated Parmesan cheese
3 tablespoons plus $^1/_2$ cup butter
1 cup whipping cream
Pepper to taste

Cook pasta according to package directions; drain and return to pot. Meanwhile, place each chicken breast between plastic wrap and pound to about $^1/_4$-inch thickness. Dip each side in the 3 tablespoons Parmesan cheese. Heat the 3 tablespoons butter in large skillet and cook chicken until golden and tender, about 3 to 4 minutes on each side. While chicken is cooking, heat the remaining $^1/_2$ cup butter and the cream (this can be done in the microwave). Add cream mixture and pepper to pasta. Add the $^2/_3$ cup Parmesan cheese; toss well to mix. Place on individual serving plates. Cut each chicken breast crosswise into narrow strips. Arrange over pasta. Serve immediately. Makes 4 servings.

Lighter Version:
1 tablespoon plus $^3/_4$ cup butter
Canned evaporated skim milk

	Cal	Pro	Carb	Fib	Fat	Sat	Chol	Sod
Regular	945	45g	47g	2g	64g	38g	257mg	804mg
Lighter	637	48g	53g	2g	25g	14g	131mg	679mg

Angel Hair Pasta With Pesto

The pesto sauce adds lots of color as well as flavor.

Top of Stove

16 ounces Angel Hair pasta
2 cups whipping cream
$1/2$ cup pesto
1 tablespoon olive oil
3 garlic cloves, minced
1 pound boneless chicken breasts, cut into narrow strips

Cook pasta according to package directions; drain and return to pot. Meanwhile, in small saucepan, bring whipping cream to a boil. Stir in pesto; remove from heat and set aside. Heat oil in a large skillet. Add garlic and saute about 1 minute. Add chicken strips; cook until lightly browned and tender, stirring frequently. Stir in pesto sauce; bring to a simmer. Add to pasta and toss to mix. Makes 6 servings.

Lighter Version:
Half and Half
8 ounces chicken
Omit the oil
Cook garlic and chicken in nonstick pan sprayed with cooking spray

	Cal	Pro	Carb	Fib	Fat	Sat	Chol	Sod
Regular	776	30g	64g	3g	44g	22g	156mg	209mg
Lighter	547	23g	65g	3g	21g	9g	57mg	194mg

Lemon Butter Chicken

This lemon flavored chicken dish will please everyone.

Oven 375°

6 chicken breast halves, skinned and boned
¹/₃ cup Dijon mustard
³/₄ cup dry Italian bread crumbs
1 lemon (you will need 1 teaspoon grated lemon peel and the juice)
³/₄ cup butter, melted
8 ounces fettuccine

Brush chicken breasts with mustard. Coat with bread crumbs and place, rounded side up, in 13x9-inch baking dish. Mix lemon juice, lemon peel and butter; pour over chicken. Bake at 375° for 45 minutes or until chicken is cooked through, basting once or twice. If chicken pieces are quite thin, you may need to reduce cooking time. Watch carefully so as not to over-cook.

Start the pasta about 15 minutes before the chicken is done, following package directions; drain thoroughly. Toss with some of the butter mixture from baking dish. Place on a large platter or individual plates and top with the chicken. Makes 6 servings.

Lighter Version:
¹/₃ cup butter

	Cal	Pro	Carb	Fib	Fat	Sat	Chol	Sod
Regular	566	35g	42g	2g	28g	15g	136mg	1030mg
Lighter	452	35g	42g	2g	15g	7g	101mg	899mg

Chicken   49

Ranch Style Pasta with Chicken

When I make this recipe, I think of my daughter-in-law Kathy. She loves Ranch dressing and their family goes through gallons of it. Well, maybe not gallons, but she buys Ranch like I buy Thousand Island.

Top Of Stove

8 ounces egg noodles
1/2 cup butter
1 (1-ounce) package Hidden Valley Original Ranch Dressing
1/2 cup peas
1/4 cup freshly grated Parmesan cheese plus 1 tablespoon
2 cups cubed cooked chicken

Cook noodles according to package directions; drain and return to pot. (If peas are frozen, add to noodles during last two minutes of cooking time.) Meanwhile, melt butter in small saucepan; add dressing mix. Add butter mixture and the 1/4 cup Parmesan cheese to the pasta and toss to coat. Add chicken and peas. Pour onto serving platter and sprinkle with remaining 1 tablespoon Parmesan cheese. Makes 4 servings.

VARIATION: Omit chicken and serve as a side dish. Will make 6 to 8 side-dish servings.

Lighter Version:
Noodles made without eggs
1/3 cup butter

	Cal	Pro	Carb	Fib	Fat	Sat	Chol	Sod
Regular	522	28g	38g	3g	29g	16g	158mg	458mg
Lighter	445	20g	48g	3g	19g	11g	69mg	351mg

Lowfat Chicken Spaghetti Dish

A colorful pasta dish.

12 ounces spaghetti, broken into thirds
3 chicken breast halves, skinned and boned
1/4 cup lite soy sauce
1 small red bell pepper, cut into strips
3 ounces fresh or frozen Chinese pea pods
Freshly ground black pepper

Cook spaghetti according to package directions; drain. Spray a large skillet with nonfat cooking spray. Cut chicken crosswise into narrow strips; add to skillet and cook over medium-high heat until chicken is tender, stirring frequently. Add soy sauce, red pepper and Chinese pea pods. Cook until peppers and pea pods are just crisp-tender. Season with pepper. Toss with noodles. Makes 6 servings.

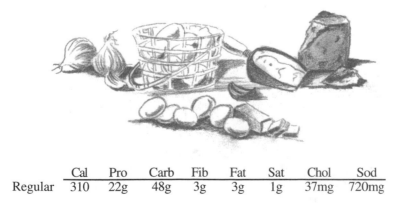

	Cal	Pro	Carb	Fib	Fat	Sat	Chol	Sod
Regular	310	22g	48g	3g	3g	1g	37mg	720mg

Chicken 51

Creamy Chicken and Noodles

A surprisingly simple recipe that will get raves every time.

Top Of Stove
Oven 350°

4 chicken breast halves, skinned and boned
1/4 cup butter
1/3 cup sliced green onions
1 can Cream of Chicken soup
Paprika
8 ounces spaghetti

Clean chicken breasts and pat dry. Place in an 11x7-inch baking dish, rounded side down. Dot chicken with butter. Bake at 350° for 15 minutes. Remove from oven and sprinkle green onion over melted butter. Turn chicken and bake 15 minutes. Remove from oven; stir soup and spread over chicken. Sprinkle lightly with paprika. Bake 15 minutes or until chicken is cooked through. Meanwhile, cook pasta according to package directions; drain. Serve chicken over spaghetti. Makes 4 servings.

Lighter Version:
2 tablespoons butter
"Healthy Request" soup

	Cal	Pro	Carb	Fib	Fat	Sat	Chol	Sod
Regular	539	37g	51g	3g	20g	10g	110mg	783mg
Lighter	467	36g	52g	3g	11g	5g	95mg	425mg

Chicken Linguine with Pesto

Because of the high fat content, pesto-type recipes should be enjoyed, but eaten in moderation.

Top Of Stove

8 ounces linguine
2 chicken breast halves, skinned and boned
1 tablespoon olive oil
1/2 cup pesto, or to taste
2 large plum tomatoes, coarsely chopped
1/4 cup freshly grated Parmesan cheese

Cook pasta according to package directions; drain. Meanwhile, cut chicken crosswise into narrow strips. Heat oil in medium skillet and cook chicken over medium-high heat, stirring frequently. Add pesto and tomatoes. Add pasta and toss to mix. Cook over low heat just until heated through. Garnish with Parmesan cheese. Makes 4 servings.

NOTE: This recipe will take on a different flavor according to the type or brand of pesto used. If purchasing pesto, you may wish to experiment with different brands, or even better, try making your own, especially during the summer when basil is abundant.

<u>Lighter Version:</u>
Omit the oil and spray a nonstick pan with cooking spray

	Cal	Pro	Carb	Fib	Fat	Sat	Chol	Sod
Regular	513	29g	48g	3g	22g	6g	50mg	363mg
Lighter	483	29g	48g	3g	19g	5g	50mg	363mg

Chicken and Fettuccini

Chicken and fettuccine goes together beautifully to make a delicious, but quick and easy, pasta dish.

8 ounces fettuccine
4 small chicken breast halves, skinned and boned
1 tablespoon olive oil
$^1/_2$ cup finely chopped onion
1 cup whipping cream
$^2/_3$ cup freshly grated Parmesan cheese

Cook pasta according to package directions; drain. Slice chicken into narrow strips; toss with olive oil. In medium skillet, saute chicken and onion until chicken is cooked through. Add cream and cook until slightly thickened, about 4 to 5 minutes. Stir in Parmesan cheese and cook over low heat until melted. Place pasta on individual servings plates and top with chicken mixture. Makes 4 servings.

VARIATION: Along with chicken and onion, add 6 ounces fresh mushrooms, red pepper strips, zucchini or yellow squash.

Lighter Version:
Three breast halves
Cook chicken in nonstick skillet sprayed with cooking spray
$^1/_2$ cup canned evaporated skim milk
$^1/_3$ cup Parmesan cheese

	Cal	Pro	Carb	Fib	Fat	Sat	Chol	Sod
Regular	671	41g	49g	3g	34g	18g	162mg	390mg
Lighter	398	34g	50g	3g	6g	2g	62mg	240mg

Chicken, Red Pepper and Noodles

Red bell pepper adds a nice texture and flavor to this delicious pasta dish.

8 ounces pasta (egg noodles, bow ties, etc)
3 chicken breast halves, skinned and boned
2 tablespoons olive oil
1 cup coarsely chopped onion
1 red bell pepper, cut into strips
1 (28-ounce) jar chunky spaghetti sauce (about 3 cups)

Cook pasta according to package directions; drain. Meanwhile, cut chicken into strips or cubes. Heat oil in a large skillet and quickly brown the chicken. Remove and set aside. Add onion and red pepper; cook until slightly softened. Add spaghetti sauce and chicken. Bring to a boil, reduce heat and simmer 10 minutes. Place noodles on serving plates and top with sauce. Makes 4 servings.

Lighter Version:
2 chicken breast halves
Cook chicken in nonstick pan sprayed with cooking spray
Pasta made without eggs

	Cal	Pro	Carb	Fib	Fat	Sat	Chol	Sod
Regular	558	32g	70g	7g	18g	3g	55mg	1093mg
Lighter	463	25g	70g	7g	10g	2g	37mg	1077mg

Fettuccine Chicken with Lemon Sauce

Can use leftover chicken, turkey, ham, beef or pork.

8 ounces fettuccine
1 teaspoon olive oil
$1/2$ cup chopped onion
$3/4$ cup whipping cream
1 teaspoon freshly grated lemon peel
1 cup cubed cooked chicken

Cook pasta according to package directions; drain and return to pot. Meanwhile, heat olive oil in small saucepan. Add onion and cook until soft. Add cream and cook over medium heat until slightly thickened. Add lemon peel and chicken and cook until heated through. Add to pasta and toss to coat. Makes 3 to 4 servings.

TIP: Can substitute orange peel for the lemon peel. If you are accustomed to a lot of salt, you may wish to add a small amount to taste.

<u>Lighter Version:</u>
Half and Half

	Cal	Pro	Carb	Fib	Fat	Sat	Chol	Sod
Regular	596	25g	63g	4g	26g	14g	118mg	55mg
Lighter	469	26g	64g	4g	11g	5g	59mg	57mg

Broccoli Chicken and Noodles

Cream of Broccoli soup adds a tremendous amount of flavor to a dish.

4 chicken breast halves
1 tablespoon olive oil
1 can Cream of Broccoli soup
1/4 cup milk
8 ounces egg noodles
1 tablespoon butter

Lightly brown chicken breasts in hot oil, turning to brown both sides. Place in 11x7-inch baking dish sprayed with nonstick cooking spray. Combine soup and milk, blending until smooth. Pour over chicken. Bake at 350° for 45 minutes or until chicken is cooked through. Meanwhile, cook noodles according to package directions; drain and toss with the butter. Place on a large serving platter. Arrange chicken over noodles and pour sauce over top. Makes 4 servings.

TIP: The chicken looks nice in this recipe whether you remove the skin before cooking or choose to leave it on.

Lighter Version:
Omit oil; brown chicken in nonstick skillet sprayed with cooking spray
Remove skin from chicken before eating
"Healthy Request" soup
Nonfat milk
Pasta made without eggs

	Cal	Pro	Carb	Fib	Fat	Sat	Chol	Sod
Regular	503	39g	40g	3g	20g	6g	141mg	355mg
Lighter	426	36g	52g	3g	7g	2g	79mg	388mg

Chicken and Broccoli

This is an entree you can prepare in about 30 minutes. If desired, omit chicken and use as a vegetable dish.

Top Of Stove

8 ounces fettuccine
2 chicken breast halves, skinned and boned
2 teaspoons olive oil
2 cups broccoli flowerets
$1/2$ cup whipping cream
$1/3$ cup freshly grated Parmesan cheese

Cook fettuccine according to package directions. Meanwhile, cut chicken into bite-size pieces and saute in olive oil until light golden in color and cooked through, stirring frequently. A couple of minutes before you think the pasta is ready, add broccoli. When done, drain and return to pot. Stir in cream and Parmesan cheese. Add chicken. Serve on attractive platter. Makes 2 main dish servings or 4 vegetable servings.

<u>Lighter Version:</u>
Omit oil
Cook chicken in nonstick skillet sprayed with cooking spray
Canned evaporated skim milk

	Cal	Pro	Carb	Fib	Fat	Sat	Chol	Sod
Regular	934	52g	97g	8g	37g	19g	168mg	416mg
Lighter	739	56g	103g	8g	10g	4g	88mg	467mg

Cornish Hens with Noodles

Serve with a salad and French bread for a delicious meal.

2 Cornish hens, halved
2 tablespoons olive oil, divided
$1/2$ teaspoon dried rosemary, crushed
1 teaspoon dried parsley
$1/4$ teaspoon paprika
8 ounces egg noodles

Place Cornish hen halves, cut side up, on a shallow baking pan sprayed with nonstick cooking spray. Combine 1 tablespoon of the olive oil, rosemary, parsley and paprika; brush mixture over hens. Bake at 350° for 45 to 60 minutes or until cooked through. Cook noodles according to package directions; drain. Serve Cornish hens on a bed of noodles that have been tossed with remaining olive oil. Makes 4 servings.

TIP: If you know your butcher, perhaps you can ask him to cut the Cornish hens in half for you.

<u>Lighter Version:</u>

Omit 1 tablespoon oil and spray Cornish hens lightly with nonstick cooking spray
Sprinkle with rosemary, parsley and paprika
Remove skin from Cornish hens before eating

	Cal	Pro	Carb	Fib	Fat	Sat	Chol	Sod
Regular	608	48g	35g	2g	29g	7g	180mg	489mg
Lighter	420	42g	35g	2g	11g	3g	156mg	404mg

Stir-Fry Noodles with Beef

*With a package of stir-fry noodles in your refrigerator, as well as some
fresh vegetables and leftover meat, you can have dinner on the table in less
than 30 minutes.*

Top Of Stove

**1 (7.7-ounces) package fresh Yakisoba Stir-Fry Noodles with Teriyaki
  Sauce
1 tablespoon oil
1 medium carrot, julienned
$^1/_2$ medium onion, sliced into narrow wedges and separated
1 cup fresh broccoli flowerets
6 ounces sirloin steak, cooked, sliced thin**

Separate noodles according to package directions. Heat oil in large skillet or
wok. Add carrots and onion; cover and cook 2 to 3 minutes. Add broccoli
and meat slices; cook 2 to 3 minutes or until vegetables are just crisp-tender.
Add noodles and $^1/_4$ cup water. Cook about 1 minute. Add sauce packet and
$^1/_4$ cup water; heat through. Makes 4 servings.

VARIATION: Substitute or add 1 or more of the following:

Pork	Celery	Peanuts	Water Chestnuts
Chicken	Mushrooms	Cashews	Chinese Pea Pods
Shrimp	Peppers	Bok Choy	

TIP: Look for the noodles in the produce department of your supermarket
or substitute cooked Chinese noodles and bottled Teriyaki Sauce.

Lighter Version:
Omit oil; cook vegetables in a small amount of water
Substitute chicken for the beef

	Cal	Pro	Carb	Fib	Fat	Sat	Chol	Sod
Regular	224	14g	27g	2g	8g	1g	24mg	378mg
Lighter	178	14g	27g	2g	2g	0g	25mg	377mg

Oriental Pasta Stir-Fry

The secret to a tender, juicy flank steak is to not overcook it. Almost any meat or seafood can be used in this recipe.

Top Of Stove

8 ounces Chinese egg noodles
1 small flank steak (about 12 ounces)
¹/₄ cup soy sauce
1 cup sliced green onions (about 4 onions)
1 carrot, julienned
1 small red pepper, cut into strips

Cook noodles according to package directions, or about 8 to 10 minutes; drain. Cut steak in half lengthwise. Then cut crosswise into thin slices, but cut the slices at an angle to make thin, but wider slices. Spray a large non-stick skillet with cooking spray. Heat skillet on high; when hot, add about ¹/₃ of the meat and cook quickly until lightly browned but with some pink showing. Remove from skillet and continue until all the meat is cooked.

Return meat to pan along with the soy sauce, green onions, carrots and red peppers. Cover and cook, over medium heat, about 3 to 4 minutes. Add noodles. Serve with additional soy sauce, if desired. Makes 4 servings.

Lighter Version:
8 ounces flank steak
Increase servings to 6

	Cal	Pro	Carb	Fib	Fat	Sat	Chol	Sod
Regular	347	26g	40g	3g	9g	3g	90mg	1104mg
Lighter	202	13g	27g	2g	4g	2g	50mg	724mg

Noodles with Veal

A main dish meal you can make in less than 30 minutes.

Top Of Stove

8 ounces spaghetti
3 tablespoons butter, divided
1 large garlic clove, minced
1 pound veal, cubed
1 cup whipping cream
1 teaspoon paprika

Cook noodles according to package directions; drain. Heat 2 tablespoons butter and the garlic in medium skillet. Add veal and brown, over medium-high heat, stirring frequently. Stir in cream and paprika. Cook over low heat about 7 to 8 minutes or until slightly thickened. (Do not boil as mixture could separate. If this should happen, stir in additional cream until smooth.) Toss spaghetti with remaining 1 tablespoon butter. Place on large platter. Make a well in center and spoon veal mixture over top. Makes 3 to 4 servings.

TIP: Do not overcook veal or meat will be tough.

Lighter Version:
1 tablespoon butter
Half and Half
•

	Cal	Pro	Carb	Fib	Fat	Sat	Chol	Sod
Regular	861	39g	62g	3g	50g	28g	261mg	252mg
Lighter	625	40g	64g	3g	22g	11g	162mg	177mg

Fontina Lasagna

This is a wonderful lasagna made with three layers of noodles, meat sauce and Fontina cheese. It was quite a hit at a taste-testing party.

Top Of Stove

12 lasagna noodles
1 pound lean ground beef
4 cups chunky spaghetti sauce with mushrooms
6 tablespoons freshly grated Parmesan cheese
5 cups (20-ounces) Fontina cheese, shredded

Cook noodles as directed on package; drain and rinse with cold water. Meanwhile, brown ground beef; drain off fat. Add spaghetti sauce and simmer while noodles are cooking.

Spread about 1/2 cup of the spaghetti sauce in a 13x9-inch baking dish sprayed with nonstick cooking spray. Place 4 of the lasagna noodles (overlapping slightly) in baking dish. Spread with about 2 cups meat sauce. Sprinkle with 2 tablespoons of the Parmesan cheese, then with 1/3 of the Fontina cheese. Repeat, making three layers and ending with the Fontina cheese. Bake at 350° for 30 minutes or until cheese is golden. Let stand 5 to 10 minutes before cutting. Makes about 8 servings.

TIP: Can be made ahead, baked and reheated. Cover with foil (to prevent cheese from burning) and bake at 350° about 20 to 30 minutes or until heated through. Or, make ahead and chill; then bake, but extend baking time 15 to 20 minutes.

<u>Lighter Version:</u>
1 pound ground chicken
2 tablespoons Parmesan cheese
12 ounces Light Mozzarella cheese

	Cal	Pro	Carb	Fib	Fat	Sat	Chol	Sod
Regular	620	38g	38g	4g	36g	18g	124mg	1339mg
Lighter	439	31g	38g	4g	18g	7g	61mg	947mg

Taco Pasta

*Taco Pasta can be eaten as is or served over tortilla chips for a nice crunch
and added flavor.*

6 ounces spiral-type pasta
1 pound lean ground beef
1 cup chopped onion
1 package taco seasoning mix
1 cup (4-ounces) Cheddar cheese, shredded

Cook pasta according to package directions; drain. Meanwhile, brown ground beef and onion in large skillet; drain off fat. Add seasoning mix and $^3/_4$ cup water. Bring to a boil; reduce heat and simmer about 10 minutes or until liquid is absorbed. Add pasta. Sprinkle cheese over top. Cover and let stand a few minutes to melt cheese. Makes 6 servings.

Lighter Version:
$^3/_4$ pound ground chicken
Lowfat Cheddar cheese

	Cal	Pro	Carb	Fib	Fat	Sat	Chol	Sod
Regular	367	24g	29g	2g	16g	8g	71mg	396mg
Lighter	275	21g	29g	2g	7g	2g	41mg	282mg

One Pot Hamburger Noodle Dish

A good stove-top standby for quick family dinners. Also convenient for camping and boating.

8 ounces rotelli
1 pound lean ground beef
$^1/_2$ cup chopped onion
1 (14$^1/_2$-ounce) can Italian Thick 'n Chunky tomato sauce
$^1/_2$ cup freshly grated Parmesan cheese
1 cup (4-ounces) medium Cheddar cheese, shredded

Cook noodles according to package directions; drain. Meanwhile, in large deep skillet, brown the ground beef and onion; drain off fat. Add tomato sauce. Bring to a boil; reduce heat and simmer 3 to 4 minutes. Add pasta. Stir in Parmesan and Cheddar cheese. Gently stir to mix. Makes 6 servings.

TIP: If you are thinking about adding salt, please taste recipe first. It is already quite salty. If you can't find Thick 'n Chunky tomato sauce; use Italian stewed tomatoes. There is a lot of meat in this dish; if desired, reduce ground beef to $^3/_4$ pound.

<u>Lighter Version:</u>
$^3/_4$ pound ground chicken
$^1/_4$ cup Parmesan cheese
Lowfat Cheddar cheese

	Cal	Pro	Carb	Fib	Fat	Sat	Chol	Sod
Regular	469	30g	39g	3g	21g	10g	77mg	670mg
Lighter	358	25g	39g	3g	11g	3g	44mg	479mg

Cincinnati Chili with Pasta

The nice thing about spaghetti is its ease of preparation and, thankfully, almost everyone likes it.

Top Of Stove

1 pound spaghetti
1 pound lean ground beef
1 cup chopped onions
1¹/₂ tablespoons chili powder
1 (28-ounce) jar chunky spaghetti sauce with mushrooms
1 cup (4-ounces) Cheddar cheese, shredded

Cook spaghetti according to package directions; drain. Meanwhile, brown ground beef and onion in large skillet; drain off fat. Add the spaghetti sauce; bring to a boil, reduce heat and simmer 10 to 15 minutes. Toss with pasta (or serve over pasta) and sprinkle with cheese. Makes 6 servings.

VARIATION: Add kidney beans to sauce or serve sauce over pasta and top with chopped onions and cheese.

<u>Lighter Version:</u>
³/₄ pound ground chicken
Omit cheese, top with chopped onion

	Cal	Pro	Carb	Fib	Fat	Sat	Chol	Sod
Regular	638	33g	77g	7g	22g	9g	71mg	871mg
Lighter	514	25g	77g	7g	12g	2g	37mg	753mg

Company Pork Tenderloin and Noodles

*Pork tenderloin makes an elegant company dish and
this one is especially easy to prepare.*

Top Of Stove
Oven 450°

2 pork tenderloins, about 1½ pounds total weight
2 tablespoons melted butter, divided
1 cup apricot preserves
¼ cup light corn syrup
2 tablespoons Grand Marnier
8 ounces egg noodles

Place tenderloins in a small shallow baking pan. Brush with 1 tablespoon
butter. Bake at 450° for 20 minutes. Combine next 3 ingredients and pour
over meat. Bake 10 to 15 minutes or until meat tests done (160°).

Meanwhile, cook pasta according to package directions; drain and toss with
remaining tablespoon of butter. Place on serving plate. Cut pork tenderloins diagonally into ½-inch slices. Overlap, arrangint two rows of meat on
top of noodles. Spoon apricot sauce over top. Makes 4 to 6 servings.

TIP: Cooking time may vary according to the size of the tenderloins. The
ones used in this recipe were rather small, ¾ pound each.

Lighter Version:
Reduce butter to 1 tablespoon
Increase servings to 6

	Cal	Pro	Carb	Fib	Fat	Sat	Chol	Sod
Regular	780	44g	106g	3g	20g	8g	164mg	190mg
Lighter	503	29g	70g	2g	11g	4g	104mg	107mg

Cheese Tortellini with Ham

Flavorful, colorful and can be ready in less than 30 minutes.

8 ounces dried cheese-filled tortellini
6 tablespoons butter
1 cup whipping cream
$^1/_3$ cup frozen peas, thawed
3 ounces Canadian bacon (5 thin round slices) cut in julienne strips
$^1/_2$ cup freshly grated Parmesan cheese

Cook tortellini according to package directions; drain. Melt butter in large skillet. Add tortellini. Stir in whipping cream, peas and Canadian bacon and bring to a boil. Remove from heat and add Parmesan cheese. Makes 4 servings.

TIP: You may prefer to use fresh tortellini rather than dried. Some adjustments may need to be made according to the size of the pasta.

Lighter Version:
Reduce butter to 3 tablespoons
Canned evaporated skim milk

	Cal	Pro	Carb	Fib	Fat	Sat	Chol	Sod
Regular	685	22g	40g	1g	49g	30g	176mg	861mg
Lighter	453	25g	45g	1g	20g	11g	74mg	824mg

Fettuccine with Ham

Fettuccine can be mixed with a variety of meats and vegetables . This version using ham and peas is especially good.

8 ounces fettuccine
1 cup whipping cream
3/4 cup freshly grated Parmesan cheese, divided
6 ounces ham, cut into narrow strips
1/2 cup frozen peas
Freshly grated black pepper, to taste

Cook pasta according to package directions; drain and return to pot. (During last 4 minutes of cooking time, add the frozen peas). In small saucepan, heat cream to boiling, reduce heat and stir in 1/2 cup of the Parmesan cheese. Add ham and cook about 1 minute. Add to pasta; season with pepper to taste. If there is a lot of liquid in the pan, heat gently for 3-4 minutes or let stand several minutes. Place on serving platter and sprinkle with remaining cheese. Makes 4 servings (or 3 generous servings).

Lighter Version
Canned evaporated skim milk
Substitute 4 ounces Canadian bacon for ham
1/3 cup, plus 4 teaspoons Parmesan cheese

	Cal	Pro	Carb	Fib	Fat	Sat	Chol	Sod
Regular	577	25g	50g	3g	30g	18g	114mg	796mg
Lighter	357	21g	55g	3g	5g	2g	19mg	505mg

Cheese with Bacon and Pasta

A deluxe macaroni and cheese dish probably enjoyed even more by adults than children.

Top Of Stove

12 ounces penne
8 ounces bacon
1 cup whipping cream
2 cups (8-ounces) medium Cheddar cheese, shredded
1/2 teaspoon Dijon mustard
Freshly ground black pepper, to taste

Cook pasta according to package directions; drain. Meanwhile, cook bacon, drain on paper towels and crumble. About half way through cooking time for pasta, heat cream in medium-heavy saucepan. When hot, reduce heat to low and add a small amount of cheese and stir until melted. Continue until all the cheese is melted and sauce is smooth. Add Dijon mustard and pepper. Place pasta in a large deep serving bowl; pour cheese sauce over the top and sprinkle with bacon. Makes 8 side-dish servings or 4 to 6 main-dish servings.

TIP: For additional color, add about 1/4 cup coarsely chopped parsley.

Lighter Version:
6 ounces bacon
Nonfat milk
Lowfat Cheddar cheese

	Cal	Pro	Carb	Fib	Fat	Sat	Chol	Sod
Regular	874	32g	70g	4g	52g	29g	157mg	691mg
Lighter	533	32g	71g	4g	13g	5g	25mg	285mg

Easy Pasta with Bacon

A quick lunch or dinner recipe.

12 ounces rotini
3/4 cup chopped onion
3/4 cup cooked crumbled bacon
2 (14 1/2-ounce) cans Chunky Tomatoes Pasta Style, with juice
Freshly ground black pepper, to taste

Cook pasta according to package directions; drain. Meanwhile, place onion in large skillet. Add water to cover; bring to a simmer and cook until onion is soft and water has evaporated (or pour off any remaining water). Add bacon and tomatoes. Cook over medium-high heat, stirring frequently until thickened, about 8 to 10 minutes. Add pepper to taste. Toss with pasta. Makes 4 servings.

VARIATION: Add sliced or coarsely chopped ripe olives and/or 1 pound lean ground beef or turkey.

Lighter Version:
Omit bacon

	Cal	Pro	Carb	Fib	Fat	Sat	Chol	Sod
Regular	825	33g	92g	8g	37g	11g	48mg	1987mg
Lighter	500	15g	91g	8g	9g	1g	0mg	1083mg

Bacon and Basil Fettuccine

A lot of flavor is packed into this fettuccine dish using just six ingredients.

Top Of Stove

8 ounces fettuccine
4 slices bacon, chopped
1/2 cup chopped green onion (about 4 onions)
1/2 cup whipping cream
1 teaspoon dried basil
1/2 cup freshly grated Parmesan cheese

Cook fettuccine according to package directions; drain. Meanwhile, cook bacon in a medium skillet, but don't drain off the fat. Add green onions; cook until soft, about 1 to 2 minutes. Add cream and cook over medium low heat until mixture thickens slightly, about 1 to 2 minutes. Add basil and Parmesan cheese. Add drained pasta and toss to coat. Makes 2 main-dish servings.

TIP: It is very important not to let the cream mixture simmer too long after adding the cheese.

Lighter Version:
2 slices bacon
Canned evaporated skim milk
1/4 cup Parmesan cheese

	Cal	Pro	Carb	Fib	Fat	Sat	Chol	Sod
Regular	845	31g	94g	6g	38g	21g	112mg	697mg
Lighter	597	28g	99g	6g	9g	4g	17mg	414mg

Spicy Sausage with Pasta

A quick family night recipe.

Top Of Stove

12 ounces spaghetti
1 (12-ounce) package hot pork sausage
1 cup chopped green pepper
1 cup finely chopped onion
1 garlic clove, minced
1 (28-ounce) jar spaghetti sauce

Cook pasta according to package directions; drain. Crumble sausage into large skillet. Add green pepper, onion and garlic. Cook over medium heat until sausage is browned; drain off fat. Add spaghetti sauce; bring to a simmer and cook about 10 minutes to blend flavors. Serve over spaghetti. Makes 4 servings.

Lighter Version:
8 ounces light turkey sausage

	Cal	Pro	Carb	Fib	Fat	Sat	Chol	Sod
Regular	684	25g	96g	9g	23g	6g	36mg	1714mg
Lighter	602	25g	96g	9g	14g	4g	30mg	1549mg

Spaghetti with Sausage and Cheese

Not too many pasta dishes reheat well, but this one is an exception.

Top of Stove

8 ounces spaghetti
1 (12-ounce) package mild sausage
¹/₂ cup Half and Half
2 tablespoons diced canned green chilies
1 cup (4-ounces) Monterey Jack cheese, shredded

Cook pasta according to package directions; drain. Meanwhile, brown sausage in large skillet over medium heat; drain off fat. Add Half and Half and bring to a boil. Remove from heat and add green chilies and cheese. Add pasta and toss quickly to mix. Makes 4 servings.

VARIATION: Use Italian, Chorizo or turkey sausage.

Lighter Version:
Light turkey sausage
Canned evaporated skim milk
Lowfat Monterey Jack cheese

	Cal	Pro	Carb	Fib	Fat	Sat	Chol	Sod
Regular	528	24g	47g	2g	27g	12g	72mg	777mg
Lighter	445	33g	49g	2g	13g	7g	67mg	902mg

Italian Sausage with Tomato Sauce

There are times when we need to have dinner on the table in less than 30 minutes; this recipe will help solve the problem.

Top Of Stove

8 ounces fettuccine or spaghetti
6 Italian sausages, about 1 pound
1 (8-ounce) can tomato paste
1 (14$^{1}/_{2}$-ounce) can beef broth (not condensed)
$^{1}/_{2}$ teaspoon dried oregano
3 tablespoons freshly grated Parmesan cheese

Cook noodles according to package directions; drain. Meanwhile, quickly brown sausages in nonstick skillet; remove and set aside. Add tomato paste, beef broth and oregano to skillet; stir well to blend. Add sausages. Bring mixture to a boil, reduce heat and simmer about 10 minutes or until mixture has thickened and sausages are cooked through. Place pasta on individual serving plates. Top with some of the sauce and 2 sausages. Sprinkle with 1 tablespoon Parmesan cheese. Makes 3 servings.

Lighter Version:
1 sausage per serving
3 teaspoons Parmesan cheese

	Cal	Pro	Carb	Fib	Fat	Sat	Chol	Sod
Regular	683	32g	75g	6g	28g	10g	69mg	2158mg
Lighter	521	23g	74g	6g	15g	5g	34mg	1583mg

Italian Sausage with Rigatoni

You get a wonderful blend of flavors with just a few simple ingredients.

Top Of Stove

8 ounces rigatoni
8 ounces Italian sausage links
1/2 cup thinly sliced leeks
1 cup fresh or frozen peas
1 cup chicken broth

Cook pasta according to package directions; drain. Remove casings from sausage. Break sausage into small pieces and place in large skillet. Add leeks. Cook until sausage is browned and cooked through; drain off fat. Add peas and chicken broth. Cook over low heat about 5 minutes. Add noodles and mix thoroughly. Makes 4 servings.

VARIATION: Add 8 ounces sliced, fresh mushrooms
Sprinkle each serving with freshly grated Parmesan cheese
Substitute 1/2 cup sliced green onions for the leeks

<u>Lighter Version:</u>
6 ounces light turkey sausage

	Cal	Pro	Carb	Fib	Fat	Sat	Chol	Sod
Regular	376	17g	52g	5g	10g	3g	24mg	582mg
Lighter	327	18g	52g	5g	5g	2g	23mg	495mg

Italian Sausage Pasta

The finished dish looks like it makes enough to feed an army. If you have just a small army to feed, make half the recipe.

Top Of Stove

16 ounces fettuccine
1 pound Italian sausage links
2 medium onions, coarsely chopped
8 ounces fresh mushrooms, sliced
1 cup whipping cream
1/2 cup freshly grated Parmesan cheese, plus 2 tablespoons

Cook fettuccine according to package directions; drain and return to pot. Meanwhile, remove casings from sausage and crumble into a large skillet. Add onion and cook until sausage is browned and onion is soft. During the last few minutes of cooking time, add mushrooms and cook, stirring frequently, until soft. Add cream and bring to a boil. Pour over pasta along with the 1/2 cup Parmesan cheese and toss to coat. Place on large serving platter or individual serving plates. Sprinkle with remaining Parmesan cheese. Makes 6 to 8 generous servings.

<u>Lighter Version:</u>
1/4 pound light turkey sausage
Canned evaporated skim milk
1/3 cup Parmesan cheese

	Cal	Pro	Carb	Fib	Fat	Sat	Chol	Sod
Regular	644	24g	66g	4g	31g	15g	95mg	711mg
Lighter	453	26g	69g	4g	8g	4g	36mg	551mg

Swiss Tuna and Noodles

A super spur-of-the-moment recipe.

12 ounces egg noodles
$1/4$ cup butter
$1/4$ cup flour
2 cups milk
$1/3$ cup Swiss or Cheddar cheese, shredded
2 ($6^{1}/_8$-ounce) cans tuna, drained

Cook noodles according to package directions; drain. Meanwhile, melt butter in medium saucepan. Stir in flour and cook, over medium heat about 1 minute. Remove from heat; add milk and stir quickly to blend. Return to heat and continue cooking, stirring frequently, until thickened. Add cheese, a small amount at a time, and stir until melted. Add tuna and let stand a couple of minutes to heat through. Serve over noodles. Makes 4 servings.

NOTE: If you use the lighter version of this recipe, you may need to add a little salt and pepper for additional flavor (or pass the salt and pepper at the table).

Lighter Version:
Nonfat milk
Lowfat Swiss or Cheddar cheese
Solid white tuna, packed in water

	Cal	Pro	Carb	Fib	Fat	Sat	Chol	Sod
Regular	572	38g	58g	3g	20g	11g	142mg	504mg
Lighter	558	40g	58g	3g	17g	9g	141mg	556mg

Brie and Pasta with Shrimp

If Brie is a favorite of yours, you will enjoy this versatile pasta dish topped with shrimp, crab or chicken.

8 ounces Angel Hair pasta
8 ounces Brie cheese, diced
1/2 cup Half and Half
2 tablespoons finely chopped parsley
Pepper to taste
8 ounces cooked shrimp (should be hot)

Cook pasta according to package directions; drain well and return to pot. Add Brie and stir until melted. Add Half and Half, parsley and pepper. Place on large serving platter or individual plates. Top with shrimp. Makes 4 servings.

TIP: If desired, serve with lemon wedges as a garnish and/or squeeze juice over shrimp.

Lighter Version:
Canned evaporated skim milk

	Cal	Pro	Carb	Fib	Fat	Sat	Chol	Sod
Regular	507	32g	46g	2g	21g	12g	178mg	499mg
Lighter	493	34g	49g	2g	17g	10g	168mg	523mg

Spaghetti and Shrimp Pasta

This makes a lot of pasta. Half the recipe would probably be enough for 4 servings.

1 pound spaghetti
1 cup butter
1 large garlic clove, minced
1 cup chopped fresh parsley
1 cup freshly grated Parmesan cheese
1 pound cooked shrimp (should be hot)

Cook spaghetti according to package directions; drain and return to pot. Meanwhile, melt butter in small saucepan. Add garlic and simmer about a minute. Stir in parsley. Pour over pasta and toss to coat. Add Parmesan cheese and toss until melted and smooth. Pour onto a "large" serving platter or deep bowl, making a slight well in center. Fill with shrimp. If desired, sprinkle shrimp with additional parsley and Parmesan cheese. Makes 6 servings.

Lighter Version:
$1/2$ cup butter
Omit the 1 cup Parmesan cheese and
sprinkle each serving with 2 teaspoons

	Cal	Pro	Carb	Fib	Fat	Sat	Chol	Sod
Regular	722	33g	61g	4g	38g	23g	243mg	800mg
Lighter	520	27g	60g	4g	18g	10g	190mg	372mg

Crab, Spinach and Fettuccine

A quick and easy pasta dish with a nice creamy mild-flavored cheese sauce.

Top Of Stove

8 ounces fettuccine
1/2 cup whipping cream
5 ounces Brie cheese, skin removed, diced
1/2 cup firmly packed shredded fresh spinach
8 ounces cooked crab, flaked (should be hot)
1/4 cup freshly grated Parmesan cheese

Cook pasta according to package directions; drain. During last 5 minutes pasta is cooking, heat whipping cream in a small saucepan. Slowly add the Brie, stirring after each addition until melted. Place pasta in large bowl. Add cheese sauce and spinach. Toss quickly to coat. Place on serving plates. Top each serving with half the crab and sprinkle with 2 tablespoons Parmesan cheese. Makes 2 servings.

Lighter Version:
Canned evaporated skim milk
6 ounces crab
2 tablespoons Parmesan cheese

	Cal	Pro	Carb	Fib	Fat	Sat	Chol	Sod
Regular	1063	60g	92g	5g	50g	29g	276mg	1038mg
Lighter	850	55g	98g	5g	25g	14g	163mg	894mg

Baked Salmon with Pesto

Salmon is a perfect choice for easy entertaining. If desired, grill the salmon and serve the pasta as a side-dish.

Top Of Stove
Oven 450°

8 ounces fettuccine
4 salmon steaks or a 16-ounce fillet
1 tablespoon butter, melted
1 tablespoon Dijon mustard
$^1/_2$ cup pesto, or to taste
Lemon wedges (optional)

Cook pasta according to package directions; drain. Place salmon in a shallow baking pan sprayed with nonstick cooking spray. Brush with butter and mustard. Bake at 450° for 10 minutes or until a wooden toothpick inserted comes out clean. Toss pasta with the pesto sauce. Place on a serving platter and arrange salmon on top. Garnish with lemon wedges, if desired. Makes 4 servings.

Lighter Version:
Omit butter on salmon
Omit pesto
Toss pasta with 1 tablespoon butter
Sprinkle with fresh chopped basil

	Cal	Pro	Carb	Fib	Fat	Sat	Chol	Sod
Regular	652	44g	47g	3g	31g	8g	115mg	411mg
Lighter	497	39g	45g	2g	17g	4g	107mg	200mg

Fettuccine with Smoked Salmon

This is an excellent recipe for those times when you want a delicious meal, but have very little time to cook.

Top Of Stove

16 ounces fettuccine
1/4 cup butter
1 cup whipping cream
1 cup freshly grated Parmesan cheese
Freshly ground black pepper
8 ounces smoked salmon, cubed or flaked

Cook pasta according to package directions; drain. Meanwhile, melt butter in a large deep skillet or wok. Add cream and heat through. Gradually add the Parmesan cheese, stirring to melt. When mixture is hot, add pasta, tossing to coat. Season with pepper to taste and add salmon. Cook over low heat about 2 minutes. There should be quite a bit of sauce in the pan, but the noodles will gradually absorb most of it. (If you would like additional color, sprinkle with chopped parsley or dill.) Makes 4 large servings.

Lighter Version:
2 tablespoons butter
Canned evaporated skim milk
4 ounces salmon
Increase servings to 6

	Cal	Pro	Carb	Fib	Fat	Sat	Chol	Sod
Regular	931	37g	92g	5g	46g	26g	145mg	1742mg
Lighter	461	24g	65g	3g	11g	6g	29mg	778mg

Spaghetti with Anchovies

A terrific pasta dish for anchovy and garlic lovers only.

8 ounces spaghetti
1/4 cup olive oil
2 large garlic cloves, minced
1 (1³/4 to 2-ounce) can anchovies, drained and chopped
1¹/2 teaspoons lemon juice
1/3 cup freshly grated Parmesan cheese

Cook pasta according to package directions; drain and return to pot. Meanwhile, heat oil in small skillet. Add garlic and cook, over low heat, about 2 minutes. Add anchovies and cook about 2 to 3 minutes. Add anchovy mixture and lemon juice to pasta and toss to mix. Serve topped with Parmesan cheese. Makes 4 side-dish servings.

TIP: Use amount of anchovies according to taste.

Lighter Version:
2 tablespoons olive oil
1/4 cup Parmesan cheese

	Cal	Pro	Carb	Fib	Fat	Sat	Chol	Sod
Regular	407	15g	46g	2g	18g	4g	17mg	611mg
Lighter	339	14g	45g	2g	11g	3g	16mg	573mg

Fillet of Sole and Noodles

Bursting in flavor and color, low in fat and also a breeze to make.

Top Of Stove

8 ounces fettuccine
4 fillets (about 1 pound) sole, orange roughy, turbot or red snapper
1 tablespoon oil
2 medium bell peppers (1 red, 1 green), cut into narrow strips
1 medium onion, sliced, separated into rings
Salt and pepper, to taste

Cook pasta according to package directions; drain and rinse briefly with water. Meanwhile, heat oil in large nonstick skillet. Add bell peppers and onion. Arrange fillets over top. Sprinkle with salt and pepper. Cover skillet and cook over medium-low heat about 10 minutes. Remove cover and continue cooking until fish flakes easily with a fork. Serve over pasta. Makes 4 servings.

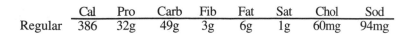

	Cal	Pro	Carb	Fib	Fat	Sat	Chol	Sod
Regular	386	32g	49g	3g	6g	1g	60mg	94mg

Linda's Spaghetti Sauce with Red Peppers

Everyone enjoys Linda's spaghetti. The mild flavor of the red pepper blends well with the spaghetti sauce giving it a slightly sweet taste.

Top Of Stove

1 pound lean ground beef
¹/₂ cup chopped onion
1 medium red pepper, coarsely chopped
4 ounces fresh mushrooms, sliced
3 cups chunky spaghetti sauce
Salt and pepper, to taste

Brown ground beef and onion in a large skillet. Add mushrooms toward end of cooking time; drain off fat. Add remaining ingredients and bring to a boil. Reduce heat and simmer 15 to 20 minutes. Makes 6 servings.

TIP: The liquid may vary according to the brand of spaghetti sauce used. If liquid in pan is too thin, increase cooking time; if too thick, add a little water, tomato juice or tomato sauce.

<u>Lighter Version:</u>
³/₄ pound ground chicken

	Cal	Pro	Carb	Fib	Fat	Sat	Chol	Sod
Regular	257	18g	16g	3g	14g	4g	51mg	694mg
Lighter	209	15g	16g	3g	10g	2g	37mg	693mg

Spaghetti and Meatball Sauce

Let's face it, on busy days, what would we do without convenience foods. With these delicious meatballs, the sauce takes on a made-from-scratch flavor.

1 pound lean ground beef
1 cup soft bread crumbs (about 2 slices bread)
3 eggs, lightly beaten
1/4 cup freshly grated Parmesan cheese
Salt and pepper, to taste
3 to 3 1/2 cups spaghetti sauce

Place ground beef in mixing bowl. Process bread in blender or food processor to make soft crumbs. Add to ground beef along with the eggs, Parmesan cheese, salt and pepper. Mix to blend. (I find this much easier to do with my hands.) Form into 18 meatballs.

Heat spaghetti sauce in large skillet; reduce to simmer. Add meatballs and baste with the sauce. Cover skillet; simmer 20 to 30 minutes or until meatballs are cooked through. You can tell when the meatballs are done by gently pressing down on the top. If it feels rather firm, they should be done. Small meatballs will take less time, large meatballs more time. Serve over spaghetti. Makes 6 servings of 3 meatballs each.

VARIATION: Wrap each meatball around a small cube of feta cheese.

Lighter Version:
1 pound ground chicken
Nonfat bread
Egg substitute

	Cal	Pro	Carb	Fib	Fat	Sat	Chol	Sod
Regular	227	21g	4g	0g	14g	5g	160mg	182mg
Lighter	212	22g	6g	0g	10g	3g	53mg	249mg

Quick Spaghetti Sauce

Serve over your choice of noodles, tortellini, spaghetti, mostaccioli, etc.

Top Of Stove

1 (12-ounce) package mild sausage
3¹/₂ cups (32-ounces) chunky-style spaghetti sauce
1 tablespoon packed light brown sugar

Lightly brown sausage in large deep skillet; drain off fat. Add spaghetti sauce and brown sugar. Bring to a simmer and cook 20 minutes to blend flavors. Serve over hot pasta. Makes 5 cups sauce.

VARIATION: Omit brown sugar and add ¹/₂ cup chopped red pepper.

<u>Lighter Version:</u>
Light turkey sausage

Per ¹/₂ c	Cal	Pro	Carb	Fib	Fat	Sat	Chol	Sod
Regular	136	5g	11g	2g	9g	2g	14mg	701mg
Lighter	119	7g	11g	2g	6g	2g	18mg	714mg

Basil Pomodoro with Fettuccine

A flavorful, low-fat chunky tomato sauce. Serve with toasted sourdough rolls and a Caesar salad.

16 ounces fettuccine
2 (14¹/₂-ounce) cans ready-cut tomatoes with juice (unseasoned)
1 tablespoon olive oil
Salt and pepper, to taste
About 6 fresh basil leaves, chopped fine
4 teaspoons freshly grated Parmesan cheese

Cook pasta according to package directions; drain. Meanwhile, in medium skillet, combine tomatoes and olive oil. Bring to a boil and cook over medium heat about 6 to 8 minutes or until slightly thickened, but with some juice still remaining in pan. Add salt and pepper to taste. Stir in basil and continue to boil 1 minute. Place pasta on individual serving plates, top with some of the sauce and sprinkle with 1 teaspoon Parmesan. Makes 4 main-dish servings.

Lighter Version:
Omit olive oil

	Cal	Pro	Carb	Fib	Fat	Sat	Chol	Sod
Regular	524	18g	98g	6g	7g	1g	2mg	430mg
Lighter	494	18g	98g	6g	3g	1g	2mg	430mg

Marinara Sauce with Pasta

This is a nice change from traditional spaghetti and mushrooms.

8 ounces rigatoni or penne
8 ounces pork sausage (mildly seasoned)
1 medium garlic clove, minced
1 (4-ounce) can chopped green chilies
16 ounces marinara sauce
3 tablespoons freshly grated Parmesan cheese, divided

Cook pasta according to directions on package; drain. Meanwhile, crumble sausage in skillet; add garlic and brown. Drain off fat. Stir in green chilies, marinara sauce and 2 tablespoons of the Parmesan cheese; cook until heated through. Toss with pasta and pour into a deep serving dish. Sprinkle with remaining 1 tablespoon Parmesan cheese. Makes 4 servings.

<u>Lighter Version:</u>
Light turkey sausage
Omit Parmesan cheese in sauce
Sprinkle with 2 teaspoons Parmesan cheese

	Cal	Pro	Carb	Fib	Fat	Sat	Chol	Sod
Regular	444	18g	59g	5g	16g	5g	28mg	1391mg
Lighter	398	19g	59g	5g	10g	4g	31mg	1345mg

Tortellini with Chunky Tomato Sauce

I have used dried pasta in most of the recipes in this cookbook with the exception of tortellini and ravioli. I think fresh or refrigerated is definitely worth the extra cost.

Top Of Stove

2 teaspoons olive oil
1 medium garlic clove, minced
2 (14.5 ounce) cans whole Italian-style tomatoes, cut up, with juice
1 tablespoon sugar
1 (9-ounce) package fresh cheese-filled spinach tortellini
¼ cup freshly grated Parmesan cheese

Heat oil in medium saucepan. Add garlic and cook slightly, but do not brown. Add tomatoes and sugar. Bring to a boil; reduce heat and simmer about 30 minutes or until thickened. Meanwhile, cook tortellini according to package directions; drain. Place tortellini on serving plates. Top with tomato sauce and sprinkle with Parmesan cheese. Makes 4 servings.

NOTE: Delicious served as a side dish or as a first course.

<u>Lighter Version:</u>
Omit oil
1 tablespoon Parmesan cheese

	Cal	Pro	Carb	Fib	Fat	Sat	Chol	Sod
Regular	190	9g	26g	2g	7g	3g	16mg	539mg
Lighter	149	7g	26g	2g	3g	1g	12mg	452mg

Tomato Sauce with Onion

An easy tomato sauce with a strong onion flavor. Plus a great nonfat version when we must watch those fat grams. Makes enough sauce for about 16-ounces pasta.

Top Of Stove

1 (28-ounce) can ready-cut tomatoes, with juice
2 small onions, sliced
1 teaspoon dried basil
Salt and pepper, to taste
3 tablespoons butter

Place first four ingredients in a large saucepan or skillet. Cook over medium-low heat, about 30 minutes or until sauce has thickened and liquid is reduced. Add butter. Carefully pour mixture into a blender and blend to desired consistency. Makes 3 cups.

Lighter Version:
Omit butter (you won't even notice the difference)

Per 1/2 c	Cal	Pro	Carb	Fib	Fat	Sat	Chol	Sod
Regular	83	1g	7g	1g	6g	4g	16mg	275mg
Lighter	32	1g	7g	1g	0g	0g	0mg	216mg

Lowfat Chunky Tomato Sauce

A simple lowfat tomato sauce recipe.

Top Of Stove

2 (14¹/2-ounce) cans diced or crushed tomatoes
¹/2 cup finely chopped onion
1 large garlic clove, minced
1¹/2 teaspoons dried thyme
1 bay leaf
Salt and pepper, to taste

Combine ingredients in medium saucepan and simmer 10 to 15 minutes or until slightly thickened. Makes about 2 cups.

TIP: Let chill overnight for a more mellow flavor. Heat and serve over spaghetti; sprinkle with freshly grated Parmesan cheese.

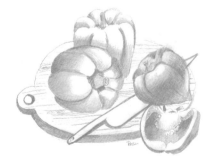

Per ¹/2 c	Cal	Pro	Carb	Fib	Fat	Sat	Chol	Sod
Regular	53	3g	12g	2g	1g	0g	0mg	347mg

Chicken Sauce Mornay

Serve over egg noodles or the short curly lasagna noodles.

Top Of Stove

2 chicken breast halves, skinned and boned
6 tablespoons butter, divided
1/4 cup flour
2 cups milk
1/2 cup (2-ounces) Swiss cheese, shredded
Salt and pepper, to taste

Slice chicken crosswise into narrow strips. Heat 2 tablespoons of the butter in a medium skillet; quickly cook chicken until tender and lightly browned.Heat the remaining 4 tablespoons butter in medium saucepan. Stir in flour until blended; heat about 1 minute until bubbly. Remove pan from heat and add milk all at one time, stirring quickly until smooth. (This is best done with a whisk.) Return to heat and continue cooking over medium heat, stirring frequently, until slightly thickened. Add cheese and stir until melted. Season with salt and pepper. Chicken should be placed over your choice of pasta and topped with the sauce. Makes 4 servings.

TIP: On a tight budget, this can be an excellent, economical dish. Purchase a whole chicken at the supermarket and use the breast for this dish and the remaining parts for another recipe.

Lighter Version:
Omit 2 tablespoons butter
Brown chicken in nonstick skillet sprayed with cooking spray
Nonfat milk
Lowfat Swiss cheese

	Cal	Pro	Carb	Fib	Fat	Sat	Chol	Sod
Regular	366	22g	12g	0g	25g	15g	105mg	306mg
Lighter	269	23g	12g	0g	14g	8g	75mg	249mg

Stroganoff Sauce

This is a wonderful Stroganoff sauce for chicken, beef or ground beef. Serve over hot buttered noodles.

Top Of Stove

Chicken or beef (see below)
6 tablespoons butter
1 cup finely chopped onions
1/4 cup flour
1³/4 cups well-seasoned chicken or beef broth
1 cup sour cream

Cut choice of meat into strips or cubes. Heat 2 tablespoons of the butter in a large skillet. Add onion and cook until soft, but do not brown. Remove from skillet and set aside. Add remaining butter to skillet. Add choice of meat and cook through. Stir in flour. Slowly add broth, stirring until smooth. Return onion to pan. Cook over medium-low heat until thickened, stirring occasionally. Reduce heat to a simmer; add sour cream and heat through, but do not boil. Serve over noodles. Makes 4 servings.

CHOICE OF MEAT: 4 chicken breast halves, boned, skinned, cubed
1¹/2 pounds tenderloin or sirloin
1 pound lean ground beef

Lighter Version:
3 chicken breast halves
3 tablespoons butter
Nonfat yogurt

	Cal	Pro	Carb	Fib	Fat	Sat	Chol	Sod
Regular	478	32g	12g	1g	33g	19g	145mg	611mg
Lighter	277	27g	15g	1g	12g	6g	79mg	523mg

Pesto Sauce

If you have lots of basil in your garden, you may wish to make and freeze several batches of pesto sauce.

1¹/₂ cups packed fresh basil leaves
¹/₃ cup pine nuts
2 medium garlic cloves
¹/₂ cup freshly grated Parmesan cheese
³/₄ cup olive oil

Combine all the ingredients in a blender or food processor and blend until smooth. Use sauce on any type of plain cooked pasta or to flavor soups or salad dressings. Cover and store in refrigerator until ready to use or freeze. Sauce will thicken as it stands. Makes 1¹/₄ cups.

TIP: May also be used as dip or as a garnish with many pasta dishes.

Per Tbs	Cal	Pro	Carb	Fib	Fat	Sat	Chol	Sod
Regular	97	2g	1g	0g	10g	2g	2mg	47mg

Sun-Dried Tomato Pesto Sauce

This recipe is for sun-dried tomato fans only. A nice, but very distinctive, tomato flavor.

3/4 cup (6-ounces) oil-packed, sun-dried tomatoes, drained
1/4 cup pine nuts
2 medium garlic cloves
1 tablespoon minced fresh basil (or 1 teaspoon dried)
1 1/2 tablespoons fresh lemon juice
1/2 cup olive oil

Blend ingredients in a food processor or blender until a nice thick sauce is formed. Toss desired amount (to taste) with pasta and sprinkle generously with freshly grated Parmesan cheese. Makes 1 1/2 cups.

Per Tbs	Cal	Pro	Carb	Fib	Fat	Sat	Chol	Sod
Regular	66	1g	4g	1g	5g	1g	0mg	149mg

Pasta with Garlic Butter Sauce

Garlic fans may wish to increase the amount of garlic used, according to taste.

Top Of Stove

8 ounces spaghetti
2 medium garlic cloves, minced
³/4 cup butter
2 tablespoons finely chopped parsley
2 tablespoons freshly grated Parmesan Cheese

Cook pasta according to package directions; drain and return to pot. Meanwhile, melt butter in medium skillet. Add garlic, bring to a simmer and cook about 1 minute to flavor the butter. Add butter and parsley to pasta and toss to coat. Pour onto serving platter. Sprinkle with Parmesan cheese. Makes 4 side-dish servings.

<u>Lighter Version:</u>
¹/4 cup butter
Increase servings to 6

	Cal	Pro	Carb	Fib	Fat	Sat	Chol	Sod
Regular	544	9g	45g	3g	37g	22g	96mg	413mg
Lighter	227	6g	30g	2g	9g	5g	22mg	119mg

Pecan Butter Sauce

*This is wonderful on pasta and equally as good served on grilled beef
tenderloin or New York steaks. Makes enough for several recipes.*

1 pound butter, softened
5 tablespoons whipping cream
3 egg yolks
1 cup freshly grated Parmesan cheese
3 medium garlic cloves, minced
1 cup toasted pecans

Cream the butter in a large mixing bowl. Add whipping cream and egg
yolks and mix until smooth. Add Parmesan cheese and garlic.Place pecans
in a food processor or blender and finely chop, but do not chop powder fine
or make a paste. Add to butter mixture and beat until well mixed. If using
immediately, add $1/2$ cup to 8 ounces cooked spaghetti, mixing to coat.
Sprinkle with Parmesan cheese.Store remainder in refrigerator or freeze.
Makes 4 cups.

NOTE: If using from the refrigerator, let stand at room temperature to soften.
If frozen, thaw and let stand at room temperature to soften. The garlic
flavor is more pronounced with freshly made but mellows after the first day.
EGGS: If you are concerned about bacterial problems with uncooked eggs,
those recipes should be avoided or see Lighter Version below.

<u>Lighter Version</u>
Substitute nonfat milk for the whipping cream
$2/3$ cup egg substitute
$3/4$ cup Parmesan cheese
$1/2$ cup toasted pecans

Per 2 Tbs	Cal	Pro	Carb	Fib	Fat	Sat	Chol	Sod
Regular	155	2g	1g	1g	16g	9g	57mg	177mg
Lighter	130	2g	1g	1g	14g	8g	33mg	171mg

Classic Alfredo Sauce

This is a wonderful and versatile pasta sauce. The basic recipe below can be tossed with pasta (enough for 1 to 1 1/2 pounds), sprinkled with Parmesan cheese and freshly ground black pepper. See Variations below.

Top Of Stove

3/4 cup butter
1 1/2 cups whipping cream
1 1/4 cup freshly grated Parmesan cheese

Heat butter and cream in medium saucepan. Cook over medium heat until mixture is hot and butter melts. Reduce heat to low; add Parmesan cheese and cook until melted and smooth, stirring constantly. Makes 6 to 8 servings.

VARIATIONS:
    Sauteed chicken or veal strips
    Sauteed fresh mushrooms and diced red or green bell pepper
    Sauteed mushrooms and zucchini slices
    Tuna chunks or salmon
    A variety of sauteed vegetables
    Artichoke hearts and chopped parsley or basil
    Sprinkle lightly with nutmeg

Enjoy!

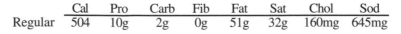

	Cal	Pro	Carb	Fib	Fat	Sat	Chol	Sod
Regular	504	10g	2g	0g	51g	32g	160mg	645mg

Gorgonzola Cheese Sauce

An excellent sauce for Gorgonzola cheese lovers.

1¹/₂ cups whipping cream
³/₄ pound Gorgonzola cheese, crumbled
¹/₄ cup toasted pine nuts

In medium saucepan, bring cream to a boil; reduce heat and bring to a simmer. Add cheese and stir until melted and sauce has thickened (lumps remaining in sauce are okay - even better). Pour sauce over desired amount of pasta. Makes enough sauce for about 12 to 16 ounces fettuccine (about 4 servings).

Enjoy!

	Cal	Pro	Carb	Fib	Fat	Sat	Chol	Sod
Regular	713	26g	5g	1g	67g	38g	197mg	1570mg

Ground Beef Soup with Orzo

Orzo is in the pasta family and looks a lot like a grain of rice. Keep a box on hand for a quick soup, vegetable or main-dish recipe.

Top of Stove

1 pound lean ground beef
1 cup chopped onion
1 (28-ounce) can whole or chopped tomatoes, with juice
3/4 cup orzo
1 1/2 cups mixed frozen vegetables (or use leftover vegetables)
Salt and pepper, to taste

In large pot, brown ground beef and onion; drain off fat. Add tomatoes. If tomatoes are whole, cut into smaller pieces. Add 6 cups water. Bring to a boil; reduce heat and simmer about 20 minutes. Bring to a boil, add orzo and vegetables. Reduce heat; add salt and pepper to taste and simmer another 20 minutes. Makes 12 cups.

<u>Lighter Version:</u>
3/4 pound ground chicken

Per Cup	Cal	Pro	Carb	Fib	Fat	Sat	Chol	Sod
Regular	113	9g	8g	2g	5g	2g	25mg	134mg
Lighter	89	8g	8g	2g	3g	1g	18mg	134mg

Chicken Oriental Soup

This is one way to get your children to eat their vegetables.

Top Of Stove

1 pound ground chicken
2 (14^1/$_2$-ounce) cans chicken broth or 3^1/$_2$ cups homemade broth
1 (10-ounce) package frozen mixed vegetables
1 (3-ounce) package oriental noodles with chicken flavor
2 tablespoons lite soy sauce

In medium skillet, brown ground chicken; drain fat. Meanwhile, pour broth into a 3-quart pot or saucepan. Add vegetables. Break up noodles and add along with the seasoning packet. Stir in soy sauce and 1^1/$_2$ cups water. Bring to a boil; add chicken. Simmer 4 to 5 minutes or until vegetables are tender. Makes 8 cups.

VARIATION: Use fresh or leftover vegetables.

Lighter Version:
^{1}/$_2$ pound ground chicken

Per Cup	Cal	Pro	Carb	Fib	Fat	Sat	Chol	Sod
Regular	171	17g	11g	2g	6g	2g	44mg	842mg
Lighter	120	11g	11g	2g	4g	1g	25mg	824mg

Beef Vegetable Soup with Pasta

Perfect for a cold winter's day. Even good without the pasta.

Top Of Stove

1 pound lean ground beef
¹/₂ cup chopped onion
2 (14¹/₂-ounce) cans Italian style stewed tomatoes, with juice
2 (14¹/₂-ounce) cans kidney beans, drained
³/₄ cup uncooked small elbow macaroni
Salt and pepper, to taste

Brown ground beef in a large pot or Dutch oven; drain off fat. Add onion, tomatoes (if large chunks, cut into smaller pieces) and kidney beans. Add 9 cups water. Bring to a boil; reduce heat and simmer about 40 minutes. Raise heat to a gentle boil, add macaroni and cook about 7 minutes or until tender, but not too soft. Add salt and pepper to taste. Makes 6 servings.

<u>Lighter Version:</u>
¹/₂ pound ground chicken

Per Cup	Cal	Pro	Carb	Fib	Fat	Sat	Chol	Sod
Regular	353	26g	39g	11g	11g	4g	51mg	752mg
Lighter	271	19g	39g	11g	5g	1g	25mg	740mg

Quick Chili Soup

*A great cold weather recipe. Add a tossed or Caesar salad, hot French
bread or hard rolls and, of course, something yummy for dessert.*

Top Of Stove

1 pound lean ground beef
1 cup chopped onion
1 (1.25-ounce) package chili mix
1 (28-ounce) can of ready-cut tomatoes
1 cup whole corn (fresh, frozen or canned)
3/4 cup uncooked elbow macaroni

In a large pot, brown ground beef and onion; drain off fat. Add chili mix,
tomatoes and 5 cups of water. Bring to a boil; reduce heat and simmer about
10 minutes. Add corn and macaroni. Cook 10 minutes or until pasta is
cooked through. Makes 6 servings.

TIP: Raid your refrigerator for any left-over vegetables you might have and
use in place of (or in addition to) the corn. Seasoning mixes are so high in
sodium I avoided adding salt to this recipe. If your taste buds are accustomed to more salt, you may wish to add a small amount or add freshly
ground pepper to increase the flavor.

Lighter Version:
3/4 pound ground chicken

Per Cup	Cal	Pro	Carb	Fib	Fat	Sat	Chol	Sod
Regular	282	20g	25g	3g	11g	4g	51mg	396mg
Lighter	234	17g	25g	3g	7g	1g	37mg	396mg

Tortellini Soup

You can't beat the warmth of a cup of hot soup on a cold day.

Top Of Stove

2 Italian sausage links (about 4 ounces)
4 cups chicken broth
4$1/2$ ounces ($1/2$ of a 9-ounce package) fresh cheese-filled tortellini
2 ounces fresh pea pods

Remove casings from sausage; break up into small pieces and brown in medium skillet; drain off fat. Meanwhile, heat chicken broth in a medium saucepan. Bring to a boil, add tortellini and continue to boil about 5 to 6 minutes. Add sausage and pea pods and cook until tortellini tests done and pea pods are crisp-tender, about 2 to 3 minutes. Makes 5 cups.

Lighter Version:
4 ounces light turkey sausage
Substitute a pasta made without eggs for the tortellini

Per Cup	Cal	Pro	Carb	Fib	Fat	Sat	Chol	Sod
Regular	113	8g	7g	0g	6g	2g	14mg	801mg
Lighter	167	11g	22g	1g	3g	1g	12mg	780mg

Vegetable Soup Italian

A sure way to get your vegetables for the day and reduce your fat grams.

Top Of Stove

1 (15-ounce) can kidney beans, drained and rinsed
1 (14$\frac{1}{2}$-ounce) can beef broth
1 (14$\frac{1}{2}$-ounce) can Italian-style stewed or chunky tomatoes
$\frac{1}{2}$ cup frozen peas
$\frac{1}{2}$ cup elbow macaroni
Salt and pepper, to taste

Place first four ingredients in a medium saucepan. Add one cup water. Bring to a boil and add macaroni. Continue to boil until pasta is tender, about 6 to 8 minutes. Add salt and pepper to taste. Makes 6 cups.

TIP: If you have any leftover vegetables, such as green beans, corn or carrots, use those to substitute (or in addition to) the peas.

VARIATION: Add $\frac{1}{2}$ pound cooked lean ground beef for a main-dish soup.

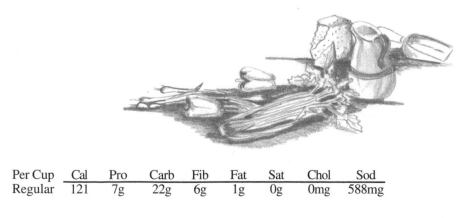

Per Cup	Cal	Pro	Carb	Fib	Fat	Sat	Chol	Sod
Regular	121	7g	22g	6g	1g	0g	0mg	588mg

Tuna Pasta Salad

Chicken, shrimp or crab may be substituted for the tuna.

8 ounces rotini or small shells
1 (6$^{1}/_{8}$-ounce) can tuna, drained
$^{3}/_{4}$ cup chopped sweet pickles
$^{1}/_{4}$ cup finely chopped onion
1 cup (4-ounces) Cheddar cheese, cubed
1 cup mayonnaise

Cook pasta according to package directions; drain and rinse thoroughly to cool. Combine with remaining ingredients. Cover and chill at least 2 hours to blend flavors. Makes 4 large servings.

VARIATION: Omit sweet pickles and add celery or chopped apples.

Lighter Version:
Solid white tuna packed in water
Lowfat cheese
Light mayonnaise

	Cal	Pro	Carb	Fib	Fat	Sat	Chol	Sod
Regular	816	26g	56g	3g	55g	13g	75mg	885mg
Lighter	509	26g	64g	3g	16g	4g	39mg	734mg

Tuna Macaroni Salad

A good standby recipe using just one can of tuna.

2 cups elbow macaroni
1 (6$^{1}/_{8}$ -ounce) can tuna, drained
2 tablespoons finely chopped onion
$^{1}/_{4}$ cup sweet pickle relish
$^{1}/_{2}$ cup frozen peas, thawed
$^{1}/_{2}$ cup mayonnaise

Cook macaroni according to package directions; drain and rinse thoroughly to cool. Combine with remaining ingredients. Cover and chill. (When ready to serve, you may need to add a little additional mayonnaise.) Makes 4 to 6 servings.

Lighter Version:
Solid white tuna, packed in water
Light mayonnaise

	Cal	Pro	Carb	Fib	Fat	Sat	Chol	Sod
Regular	383	16g	29g	2g	23g	3g	29mg	433mg
Lighter	267	16g	33g	2g	8g	1g	26mg	454mg

Chicken Pasta Salad

*A popular dish for a picnic or potluck meal. For a really quick salad, use
leftover chicken, seafood, or meat.*

Top Of Stove
Chill

8 ounces rigatoni
2 cups cubed cooked chicken
³/4 cup (3-ounces) Cheddar or Swiss cheese, shredded
¹/2 cup chopped celery
³/4 cup green peas
1 cup mayonnaise

Cook pasta according to package directions; drain and rinse thoroughly to
cool. Combine first five ingredients in large mixing bowl. Add mayonnaise
to coat. Cover and chill until ready to serve. Makes 4 large servings.

VARIATION: Cut cheese into small cubes
Omit peas and celery and use artichoke hearts and onion
Use half mayonnaise and half sour cream
Substitute tuna for the chicken

Lighter Version:
1 cup chicken
Lowfat Cheddar or Swiss cheese
Light mayonnaise

	Cal	Pro	Carb	Fib	Fat	Sat	Chol	Sod
Regular	826	34g	51g	4g	54g	12g	105mg	503mg
Lighter	477	24g	60g	3g	16g	3g	45mg	351mg

Chicken Mandarin Salad

This makes a wonderful luncheon salad. Serve with
thick slices of date bread and ice tea.

8 ounces rotini or penne
2 cups cubed cooked chicken
1 can mandarin oranges, drained
1 cup thinly sliced celery
1 (6-ounce) container orange yogurt
3/4 cup cashews, split

Cook pasta according to package directions; drain and rinse thoroughly to cool. In large bowl, combine pasta with chicken, oranges, celery and yogurt. Cover and chill until ready to serve. Just before serving, add cashews. Makes 4 to 6 servings.

TIP: If noodles absorb too much of the dressing, you may wish to add additional yogurt or a small amount of mayonnaise.

<u>Lighter Version:</u>
Nonfat yogurt
Omit cashews

	Cal	Pro	Carb	Fib	Fat	Sat	Chol	Sod
Regular	572	39g	69g	4g	16g	4g	67mg	274mg
Lighter	420	35g	60g	3g	4g	1g	66mg	114mg

Zucchini Tomato Pasta Salad

Make this salad a complete meal by adding delicious homemade muffins
and ice cream for dessert.

Top Of Stove
Chill

8 ounces linguine
2 small zucchini
8 small plum tomatoes
2 tablespoons oil-packed, sun-dried tomatoes plus 2 tablespoons of the oil
2 teaspoons balsamic vinegar
Salt and pepper, to taste

Cook pasta according to package directions; drain and rinse thoroughly to cool. Meanwhile, cut zucchini in half length-wise and then into $1/4$-inch slices. Cut tomatoes into $1/4$-inch slices. Place zucchini and tomato slices in large mixing bowl. Chop sun-dried tomatoes and add along with the oil and balsamic vinegar. Sprinkle with salt and pepper to taste. Add pasta. Let stand at room temperature for about an hour or cover and chill until ready to serve. Makes 6 servings as a side dish.

Lighter Version:
Reduce oil to 1 tablespoon

	Cal	Pro	Carb	Fib	Fat	Sat	Chol	Sod
Regular	216	6g	35g	3g	6g	1g	0mg	21mg
Lighter	197	6g	35g	3g	4g	1g	0mg	21mg

Pesto Salad

A rather simple salad with a lot of flavor.

Top Of Stove

8 ounces spiral-type pasta
$1/4$ cup sliced black olives
1 small red pepper (about $3/4$ cup chopped)
$1/4$ cup pesto, or to taste
$1/2$ cup mayonnaise
Freshly ground black pepper, if desired

Cook pasta according to package directions; drain and rinse thoroughly to cool. Place remaining ingredients in mixing bowl. Add pasta and toss to coat. Cover and chill until ready to serve. Makes 4 servings.

VARIATION: Substitute chopped plum tomatoes or halved cherry tomatoes for the red pepper.

Lighter Version:
Light mayonnaise
Increase servings to 6

	Cal	Pro	Carb	Fib	Fat	Sat	Chol	Sod
Regular	512	11g	48g	3g	31g	5g	21mg	338mg
Lighter	258	7g	35g	2g	10g	2g	8mg	224mg

Pasta Herb Salad

*Leftover pasta salad is great to take to work the next day or as a
nutritional snack for the kids.*

Top Of Stove
Chill

4 ounces rotini (about 2 cups)
1 small carrot, grated
1/3 cup Berstein's Creamy Herb & Garlic Italian Dressing
1/3 cup sliced almonds

Cook pasta according to package directions; drain. Rinse thoroughly to cool.
Combine pasta with grated carrot and the dressing. Cover and chill. Just
before serving, add almonds and additional dressing, if needed. Makes 4 to
6 servings.

TIP: If you aren't fortunate enough to find Berstein dressings in your
supermarket, use your choice of Italian dressings.

<u>Lighter Version:</u>
Lowfat dressing
2 tablespoons almonds

	Cal	Pro	Carb	Fib	Fat	Sat	Chol	Sod
Regular	259	6g	27g	2g	25g	3g	1mg	236mg
Lighter	157	5g	26g	3g	4g	0g	1mg	163mg

Macaroni Olive Salad

A nice picnic-type salad. Serve with grilled hamburgers or hot dogs.

Top Of Stove
Chill

1³/4 cups (7-ounces) elbow macaroni
2 hard-cooked eggs
2 tablespoons thinly sliced green onions
¹/2 cup finely diced celery
20 green olives, halved
1 cup mayonnaise

Cook macaroni according to package directions; drain. Rinse with cold water to cool. Combine with eggs, onion, celery and olives. Add ¹/2 cup of the mayonnaise and toss to coat. Cover and chill. When ready to serve, add enough of the remaining mayonnaise to moisten. Makes 6 servings.

Lighter Version:
Egg whites only
Light mayonnaise

	Cal	Pro	Carb	Fib	Fat	Sat	Chol	Sod
Regular	435	7g	28g	2g	33g	5g	92mg	551mg
Lighter	246	6g	34g	2g	10g	2g	10mg	345mg

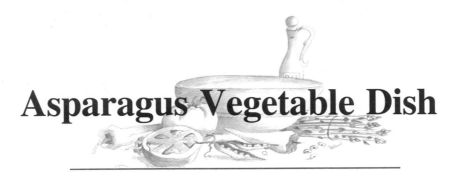

Asparagus Vegetable Dish

At the first signs of asparagus in the supermarket, or perhaps in your very own garden, try this quick and flavorful vegetable dish.

Top Of Stove

8 ounces rigatoni or mostaccioli
1 pound fresh asparagus, sliced diagonally into 1-inch pieces
3 tablespoons olive oil
$1/3$ cup finely chopped sun-dried tomatoes, packed in oil
Salt and pepper, to taste
Parmesan cheese (optional)

Cook pasta according to package directions; drain. Meanwhile, cook asparagus until just crisp-tender (use steam, microwave or water method). In large skillet, heat oil and cook sun-dried tomatoes 1 to 2 minutes, stirring frequently. Watch carefully to prevent burning. Add pasta and asparagus and toss to coat. Sprinkle with grated Parmesan cheese, if desired. Makes 6 side-dish servings.

TIP: This makes quite a lot, so unless you are a really big pasta eater, or you have a family of, say, 2 adults and 2 small children, I would suggest making just half a recipe. If you are serving a lot of food, this will probably make more than 6 servings.

VARIATION: Substitute broccoli or artichoke hearts for the asparagus.

<u>Lighter Version:</u>
2 tablespoons oil

	Cal	Pro	Carb	Fib	Fat	Sat	Chol	Sod
Regular	231	7g	35g	3g	8g	1g	0mg	100mg
Lighter	211	7g	35g	3g	5g	1g	0mg	100mg

Onions and Peppers with Rigatoni

This is quite a colorful pasta dish. Serve wth pork chops,
chicken or hamburgers.

Top Of Stove

8 ounces rigatoni
1¹/₂ tablespoons olive oil
4 cups (about 2 large onions), sliced and separated into rings
2 cups (about 1¹/₂ medium) red bell peppers, cut into narrow strips
1 cup chicken broth
Salt and pepper, to taste

Cook rigatoni according to package directions; drain. Meanwhile, heat oil in large skillet. Add onion rings; cook over medium low heat until tender and lightly browned, about 20 minutes. Add pepper strips and chicken broth. Bring to a boil; reduce heat and simmer until peppers are just crisp-tender, about 3 to 4 minutes. Season with salt and pepper. Place pasta on serving plate; top with onion-pepper mixture. Makes 4 servings.

<u>Lighter Version:</u>
Reduce oil to 2 teaspoons and use nonstick skillet

	Cal	Pro	Carb	Fib	Fat	Sat	Chol	Sod
Regular	345	11g	60g	6g	7g	1g	0mg	201mg
Lighter	320	11g	60g	6g	4g	1g	0mg	201mg

Mostaccioli with Sun-Dried Tomatoes

My son, Mike, gave me a beautiful Italian Pasta gift basket for Christmas and the first item I used was the jar of sun-dried tomatoes. They were wonderful in this recipe.

Top Of Stove

8 ounces mostaccioli
$^1/_4$ cup oil-packed, sun-dried tomatoes, plus 1 tablespoon of the oil
1 (6$^1/_2$-ounce) jar marinated artichoke hearts, coarsely chopped

Cook pasta according to package directions; drain. Meanwhile, chop tomatoes and place in a large serving bowl. Add the 1 tablespoon oil. If you don't have enough oil, add olive oil to make up the difference. Add artichoke hearts. Add pasta and toss to coat. Serve immediately. Makes 6 side-dish servings.

TIP: This pasta dish is best served immediately after mixing or serve chilled as a delicious pasta salad. It is not as good reheated.

	Cal	Pro	Carb	Fib	Fat	Sat	Chol	Sod
Regular	218	6g	34g	4g	7g	1g	0mg	189mg

Fettuccine with Vegetables

*A colorful vegetable pasta dish or for a delicious main course, add cooked
beef, pork, ham, sausage or chicken.*

Top Of Stove

12 ounces fettuccine
2 tablespoons olive oil
2 medium garlic cloves, minced
2 medium-small zucchini, julienned
3 medium carrots
¹/₂ cup freshly grated Parmesan cheese

Cook pasta according to package directions; drain. Meanwhile, heat olive
oil and garlic in large skillet. Add zucchini and carrot strips, stirring to
coat. When simmering, cover and cook about 4 minutes or until vegetables
are crisp-tender. Add pasta. Pour onto serving platter. Sprinkle with
Parmesan cheese. Makes 6 servings.

VARIATION: If using as a main dish, will make 4 generous servings.

Lighter Version:
1 tablespoon oil
Omit Parmesan cheese and season with salt and pepper

	Cal	Pro	Carb	Fib	Fat	Sat	Chol	Sod
Regular	318	11g	54g	5g	7g	2g	3mg	101mg
Lighter	299	9g	54g	5g	6g	1g	0mg	23mg

Vegetable Noodle Side Dish

*A delicious and colorful way to use up leftover broccoli,
asparagus or zucchini.*

Top Of Stove

8 ounces medium noodles
2 tablespoons olive oil
1¹/₂ cups broccoli flowerets, cooked crisp-tender
Freshly ground black pepper
¹/₃ cup plus 1 tablespoon freshly grated Parmesan cheese
2 small plum tomatoes

Cook noodles according to package directions; drain and return to pot. Meanwhile heat olive oil in small skillet. Add broccoli and cook briefly, just long enough to heat through. Pour over noodles and toss to coat. Add pepper to taste and the ¹/₃ cup Parmesan cheese; toss to melt. Pour onto a large platter. Cut tomatoes crosswise into narrow slices and place around outer edge of the noodles. Sprinkle with remaining tablespoon Parmesan cheese. Makes 4 to 6 servings.

Lighter Version
1 tablespoon oil

	Cal	Pro	Carb	Fib	Fat	Sat	Chol	Sod
Regular	304	12g	38g	3g	12g	3g	53mg	204mg
Lighter	312	13g	48g	4g	8g	3g	8mg	196mg

Tri-Color Pasta with Peppers

Impress your guests with this colorful year-round dish that can be made in less than 20 minutes. The red and green colors also make a nice holiday buffet dish.

Top Of Stove

8 ounces tri-color, spiral-type pasta
3 tablespoons butter
1 small red pepper (about 1 cup), cut into narrow strips
¼ cup coarsely chopped pecans

Cook pasta according to package directions. Meanwhile, during last five minutes of cooking time, melt butter in small skillet. Add pecans and peppers and quickly saute until pecans are slightly toasted and peppers are crisp-tender (this doesn't take long). Drain noodles; toss with butter mixture. Makes 4 servings.

<u>Lighter Version:</u>
2 tablespoons butter
3 tablespoons finely chopped pecans

	Cal	Pro	Carb	Fib	Fat	Sat	Chol	Sod
Regular	353	8g	47g	3g	15g	6g	23mg	90mg
Lighter	315	8g	47g	3g	11g	4g	16mg	61mg

Sun-Dried Tomatoes and Peas with Pasta

The sun-dried tomatoes lend a nice tart flavor to this dish.

Top Of Stove

8 ounces Angel Hair pasta
1/2 cup frozen peas
1/4 cup oil-packed, sun-dried tomatoes, plus 2 tablespoons of oil
1 large garlic clove, minced
1/4 teaspoon dried basil
1/3 cup freshly grated Parmesan cheese

Cook pasta according to package directions, adding frozen peas last two minutes of cooking time; drain and return to pot. Meanwhile, measure out the 2 tablespoons of oil and pour into a small skillet. Add garlic to the heated oil and cook about 2 minutes (do not brown). Remove from heat. Chop tomatoes and add to skillet along with the basil; pour over pasta and toss. Sprinkle with Parmesan cheese and toss to melt. Makes 4 side-dish servings.

	Cal	Pro	Carb	Fib	Fat	Sat	Chol	Sod
Regular	366	13g	51g	4g	12g	3g	6mg	210mg

122　　Vegetables

Poppy Seed Noodles

A nice accompaniment to most entrees.

8 ounces egg noodles
2 tablespoons butter
1/2 cup frozen peas, cooked
1/2 teaspoon poppy seeds
Salt and pepper, to taste

Cook noodles according to package directions; drain and place in large serving bowl. Add butter and toss to melt. Stir in peas, poppy seeds and salt and pepper to taste. Makes 4 side-dish servings.

Lighter Version:
1 tablespoon butter
Increase servings to 6

	Cal	Pro	Carb	Fib	Fat	Sat	Chol	Sod
Regular	253	8g	37g	3g	8g	4g	61mg	86mg
Lighter	168	5g	25g	2g	5g	3g	41mg	57mg

Pasta with Bread Crumbs

If you haven't had pasta with toasted bread crumbs, you are in for a treat.

Top Of Stove

8 ounces spaghetti
$1/2$ cup olive oil
2 large garlic cloves, minced
$1/2$ cup purchased Italian-Style bread crumbs
Freshly ground black pepper
3 tablespoons freshly grated Parmesan cheese

Cook spaghetti according to package directions; drain. Meanwhile, heat oil in a large deep skillet. Add garlic and saute 2 to 3 minutes. Stir in bread crumbs and brown over medium-low heat, stirring frequently. Don't turn your back during this step or the bread crumbs could burn. Add drained pasta and stir quickly to coat. Add pepper to taste. Pour onto a large, heated platter. Sprinkle with Parmesan cheese. Serve immediately. Makes 4 side-dish servings.

	Cal	Pro	Carb	Fib	Fat	Sat	Chol	Sod
Regular	539	12g	56g	2g	30g	5g	4g	487mg

Pasta with Pine Nuts and Raisins

The raisins add a slightly sweet taste to this recipe.

8 ounces spaghetti
1/4 cup olive oil
1/4 cup pine nuts
2 large garlic cloves, minced
1/4 cup raisins
Freshly ground black pepper, to taste

Cook pasta according to package directions; drain. Meanwhile, heat olive oil in large skillet. Add pine nuts and saute until they have just a light touch of brown color; add garlic and saute until pine nuts are golden (you don't want to brown the garlic). Add pasta, raisins and pepper to taste. Makes 4 side-dish servings.

VARIATION: I like freshly grated Parmesan cheese on almost all pasta dishes and this is no exception.

Lighter Version:
Brown 2 tablespoons pine nuts in nonstick skillet (no oil)
Add 2 tablespoons oil along with garlic and heat through
Toss with pasta and raisins

	Cal	Pro	Carb	Fib	Fat	Sat	Chol	Sod
Regular	414	10g	54g	3g	19g	3g	0mg	3mg
Lighter	333	9g	53g	3g	10g	1g	0mg	3mg

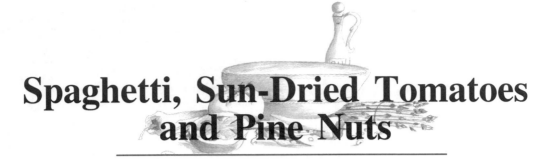

Spaghetti, Sun-Dried Tomatoes and Pine Nuts

This easy-to-make pasta dish is great anytime. Serve as a meatless dish for a light lunch or supper.

Top Of Stove

8 ounces spaghetti
¹/₂ cup oil-packed, sun-dried tomatoes, plus 4 tablespoons of oil
2 small garlic cloves, minced
¹/₄ teaspoon dried crushed red pepper, to taste
¹/₂ cup freshly grated Parmesan cheese
¹/₄ cup toasted pine nuts

Cook spaghetti according to package directions; drain. Meanwhile, coarsely chop the sun-dried tomatoes. Heat the oil in a small skillet. Add tomatoes, garlic and red pepper. Saute, about 2 minutes or until garlic is soft. Place spaghetti in large serving bowl. Add oil mixture and toss to coat. Add Parmesan cheese and nuts. Makes 6 side-dish servings or 4 main-dish servings.

TIP: If you have continued to add olive oil to the jar to keep the sun-dried tomatoes covered, you should have 4 tablespoons oil. If not, you may need to add additional olive oil to the recipe.

Lighter Version:
2 tablespoons oil
¹/₂ cup Parmesan cheese
Omit the pine nuts

	Cal	Pro	Carb	Fib	Fat	Sat	Chol	Sod
Regular	336	11g	36g	3g	18g	4g	7mg	207mg
Lighter	231	6g	35g	3g	8g	1g	0mg	56mg

Cauliflower Pasta Dish

*The mild flavor of the cauliflower blends well with
the rest of the ingredients.*

6 ounces rotini
2 teaspoons crushed rosemary
2 cups cauliflower flowerets
¹/4 cup toasted slivered almonds
2 teaspoons olive oil
Salt and pepper, to taste

Cook pasta according to package directions, adding rosemary to the water.
Add cauliflower during last 4 minutes of cooking time. Cook until pasta
tests done and cauliflower is tender; drain well. Return to pan and toss
with the oil, salt and pepper. Makes 4 side-dish servings.

TIP: It is easy to overcook the cauliflower. If desired, steam or microwave
to cook.

VARIATION: Substitute broccoli, zucchini or carrots for the cauliflower. If
using carrots, steam carrots until crisp-tender and add along with the oil.

Lighter Version:
2 tablespoons almonds
1 teaspoon olive oil

	Cal	Pro	Carb	Fib	Fat	Sat	Chol	Sod
Regular	181	6g	24g	3g	7g	1g	0mg	9mg
Lighter	146	5g	23g	2g	4g	0g	0mg	9mg

Casseroles

Baked Macaroni and Cheese

Macaroni and cheese makes a filling meatless-type dish that is rich and packed with flavor.

Top Of Stove
Oven 350°

2¹/₂ (10 ounces) elbow macaroni
2 eggs
2 teaspoons dry mustard
¹/₈ teaspoon pepper
2 cups Half and Half
4 cups (16 ounces) Cheddar cheese, shredded

Cook macaroni according to package directions; drain. Meanwhile, in large mixing bowl, combine eggs, dry mustard, pepper and Half and Half. Stir in cheese. Add macaroni and mix well. Pour into a 2¹/₂-quart deep casserole dish sprayed with nonstick cooking spray. Bake at 350° for 35 to 40 minutes or until golden and custard is set. Makes 6 to 8 servings.

	Cal	Pro	Carb	Fib	Fat	Sat	Chol	Sod
Regular	619	30g	42g	2g	37g	22g	180mg	524mg

Egg Tortilla Casserole

A delightfully different scrambled egg dish served as a casserole.

Top Of Stove
OVEN 350°

8 eggs, lightly beaten
²/3 cup milk
¹/4 of a medium green pepper, cut into narrow strips
2 cups (8-ounces) Monterey Jack cheese with jalapeno, shredded, divided
6 (8-inch) flour tortillas
³/4 cup mild salsa (optional)

Combine eggs and milk. Pour into a heated medium-size skillet sprayed with nonstick cooking spray. Add green pepper strips. Cook over medium heat, stirring as eggs begin to set around the edges. Continue to scramble eggs until cooked through, but still moist. Remove from heat. Spoon ¹/6 of the egg mixture down center of each tortilla. Sprinkle half of the cheese over eggs. Roll tortillas carefully and tightly around egg mixture. Place seam-side down in 8x8-inch baking dish sprayed with nonstick cooking spray. Sprinkle with remaining cheese. Bake at 350° for 20 minutes. Serve topped with salsa, if desired. Makes 6 servings.

NOTE: This is a little on the hot side. If desired, use regular Monterey Jack cheese. Good reheated, but if reheating in the microwave, watch carefully so as not to overcook the eggs.

Lighter Version:
Nonfat milk
Light Mozzarella cheese
Lowfat tortillas

	Cal	Pro	Carb	Fib	Fat	Sat	Chol	Sod
Regular	375	22g	24g	1g	21g	10g	318mg	584mg
Lighter	292	23g	20g	4g	14g	7g	310mg	786mg

Cheese Enchiladas

Cheese lovers will enjoy this casserole. Add a relish tray, a tossed salad and a yummy dessert to round out the meal.

Oven 350°

6 (8-inch) flour tortillas
3 cups (12-ounces) Monterey Jack cheese, shredded
$1/4$ cup butter
$1/4$ cup flour
2 cups chicken broth
1 cup (4-ounces) Monterey Jack cheese with jalapeno, cubed

Fill each tortilla with $1/2$ cup shredded Monterey Jack cheese. Roll up tight. Place in 8x8-inch baking dish (it will be tight) sprayed with nonstick cooking spray. Melt butter in medium saucepan. Stir in flour, blending until smooth. Cook until bubbles start to form. Remove from heat and stir in broth, mixing until smooth. Cook over low heat until thickened. Add a few cubes of jalapeno pepper cheese at a time; stir until melted. Continue until all the cheese has been added. Pour over tortillas. Bake at 350° for 60 minutes. Cover with foil and let stand 5 to 10 minutes before serving. Makes 6 servings.

TIP: If using a $14^1/2$-ounce can of chicken broth, add water to make 2 cups. Best served same day made.

Lighter Version:
Lowfat tortillas
Use all lowfat Monterey Jack cheese and
omit Monterey Jack cheese with jalapeno
$1/4$ cup chopped green chilies

	Cal	Pro	Carb	Fib	Fat	Sat	Chol	Sod
Regular	499	24g	25g	1g	33g	16g	88mg	910mg
Lighter	430	29g	24g	1g	24g	13g	74mg	1159mg

Baked Cheddar Egg Dish

An easy way to serve several people and equally as easy for a brunch dish.
Add sausages, fresh fruit and an assortment of pastries or muffins.

OVEN 325°

2 cups (8 ounces) medium Cheddar cheese, shredded
1 cup Half and Half
1/2 teaspoon salt
1/4 teaspoon black pepper
2 teaspoons prepared mustard
12 eggs, lightly beaten

Place cheese in 13x9-inch baking dish sprayed with nonstick cooking spray. Combine Half and Half , salt, pepper and mustard. Pour half of the mixture over the cheese. Pour eggs over top, then add the remaining milk mixture. Bake at 325° for 30 to 35 minutes or until set. Makes 6 servings.

VARIATION: Use all Swiss cheese or half Swiss and half Cheddar.

Lighter Version:
Lowfat Cheddar cheese
Canned evaporated skim milk
Egg substitute

	Cal	Pro	Carb	Fib	Fat	Sat	Chol	Sod
Regular	355	23g	4g	0g	27g	14g	479mg	573mg
Lighter	200	27g	6g	0g	7g	3g	11mg	467mg

Green Chilies Casserole

A great casserole for a brunch or lunch and the pineapple adds a nice touch. Serve with cinnamon rolls, juice and coffee. If you have my Chicken cookbook, Kathy's Cinnamon Rolls are to die for.

OVEN 350°

6 eggs
1 1/2 cups Half and Half
1/4 cup canned diced green chilies
2 cups (8-ounces) Cheddar cheese, shredded
4 slices canned pineapple, drained
1 tablespoon freshly grated Parmesan cheese

In large mixing bowl, combine eggs and Half and Half. Add chilies and Cheddar cheese; pour into a 8x8-inch baking dish sprayed with nonstick cooking spray. Bake at 350°for 30 minutes. Remove from oven; top with pineapple slices. Sprinkle with Parmesan cheese. Return to oven and bake 10 to 15 minutes or until golden and custard is set. Makes 4 servings.

TIP: Can reheat, but best served hot from the oven.

<u>Lighter Version:</u>
Egg substitute
Nonfat milk
Lowfat Cheddar cheese

	Cal	Pro	Carb	Fib	Fat	Sat	Chol	Sod
Regular	0	45g	65g	5g	21g	5g	88mg	872mg
Lighter	0	45g	65g	5g	14g	5g	88mg	872mg

Mexican Quiche

Forms a nice bread-like crust.

Oven 350°

8 eggs
¹/₄ cup flour
1 teaspoon baking powder
2 cups (8-ounces) Monterey Jack cheese, shredded
¹/₄ cup butter, melted
¹/₄ to ¹/₃ cup canned diced green chilies

Place eggs in large mixing bowl; beat to mix. Stir in flour and baking powder. Fold in cheese. Add butter and green chilies. Pour into a 10-inch quiche dish sprayed with nonstick cooking spray. Bake at 350° for 30 to 35 minutes or until custard is set. Let stand 5 minutes before cutting. Makes 6 servings.

VARIATION: Use chopped red and green pepper for the green chilies.
          Serve topped with salsa

Lighter Version:
Egg substitute
Lowfat Monterey Jack cheese
1 tablespoon butter

	Cal	Pro	Carb	Fib	Fat	Sat	Chol	Sod
Regular	329	18g	6g	0g	26g	14g	337mg	510mg
Lighter	211	19g	6g	0g	11g	7g	26mg	408mg

Quiche Lorraine

This popular dish is great served with a nice tossed salad and fresh fruit.

1 (9-inch) pie shell
1 pound bacon, cooked and crumbled
2 cups (8-ounces) Swiss cheese, shredded
5 eggs, lightly beaten
1 cup Half and Half

Place half the bacon in pie crust. Sprinkle with half of the cheese. Repeat layers. Combine eggs and Half and Half and thoroughly blended. Pour over cheese. Bake at 350° for 40 to 45 minutes or until custard is set and knife inserted in center comes out clean. Let stand 5 minutes before cutting. Makes 6 servings.

TIP: To prevent a soggy crust, you may wish to partially prebake the crust. Prick crust with fork and bake at 400° about 8 to 10 minutes. Cool.

Enjoy!

	Cal	Pro	Carb	Fib	Fat	Sat	Chol	Sod
Regular	558	27g	18g	1g	42g	18g	247mg	726mg

Janice's Impossible Quiche

Janice is a wonderful cook and this is one of my most frequently used recipes. A favorite Christmas brunch is: Quiche, a spicy sausage dish, fruit salad and cinnamon rolls.

Oven 350°

3 eggs
1/2 cup baking mix
1/4 cup butter
1 1/2 cups milk
1/2 cup (2 ounces) cubed ham
1 cup (4 ounces) Cheddar cheese, shredded

Place eggs, baking mix, butter and milk in a food processor or blender and process until smooth. Pour into a 9-inch pie pan sprayed with nonstick cooking spray. Sprinkle with ham, then cheese. Press mixture down into milk. Bake at 350° for 40 to 45 minutes or until knife inserted in center comes out clean. Let stand 5 to 10 minutes fore cutting. Makes 6 servings.

Lighter Version
Egg substitute
3 tablespoons butter
Nonfat milk
Canadian bacon
Lowfat Cheddar cheese

	Cal	Pro	Carb	Fib	Fat	Sat	Chol	Sod
Regular	269	13g	10g	0g	20g	11g	156mg	510mg
Lighter	190	13g	10g	0g	10g	5g	26mg	421mg

Hamburger Quiche

When you don't know what to fix for breakfast, lunch or dinner - make a Quiche!

Top Of Stove
Oven 350°

$^{1}/_{2}$ **pound lean ground beef**
1$^{1}/_{2}$ cups (6-ounces) Swiss cheese, shredded
1 (9-inch) pie shell, unbaked
$^{2}/_{3}$ **cup milk**
1 tablespoon cornstarch
3 eggs, lightly beaten

Brown ground beef; drain off fat. Meanwhile, sprinkle cheese in pie shell. Top with ground beef. Combine milk and cornstarch, beating slightly to blend. Add eggs and mix thoroughly. Pour into pie shell. Bake at 350° (reduce to 325° if using a glass dish) for 35 to 40 minutes or until custard is set and top is lightly browned. Makes 6 servings.

TIP: Not as good reheated.

Lighter Version:
$^{1}/_{2}$ pound ground chicken
Lowfat Swiss cheese
Nonfat milk
Egg substitute

	Cal	Pro	Carb	Fib	Fat	Sat	Chol	Sod
Regular	395	22g	18g	1g	26g	11g	159mg	299mg
Lighter	317	22g	18g	1g	16g	5g	35mg	327mg

Chicken Broccoli Quiche

A nice creamy quiche dish. Serve with a fresh fruit salad on a bed of lettuce and hard rolls. Also good reheated.

Top Of Stove
Oven 350°

1 (9-inch) pie shell
2 cups broccoli flowerets
1 cup (4-ounces) Swiss cheese, shredded
1 cup cubed cooked chicken breast
2 eggs, lightly beaten
1 cup whipping cream

Broccoli should be steamed until just-crisp tender. Place in pie shell. Sprinkle with cheese. Add chicken. Combine eggs and cream, beating with a fork until well mixed. Pour into pie shell. Slightly press down on the ingredients to cover with as much cream mixture as possible. Bake at 350° for 40 to 50 minutes or until custard is set. Let stand 5 to 10 minutes before cutting. Makes 6 servings.

Lighter Version
Lowfat Swiss cheese
Egg substitute
Half and Half

	Cal	Pro	Carb	Fib	Fat	Sat	Chol	Sod
Regular	426	16g	18g	1g	33g	16g	156mg	266mg
Lighter	297	17g	18g	1g	17g	6g	36mg	283mg

Chicken and Potato Quiche

*This hearty quiche can be prepared quickly and left-overs,
if any, are good reheated.*

Oven 350°

1 (9-inch) pie shell, unbaked
1 cup (4-ounces) Swiss cheese, shredded
1 cup cubed cooked chicken
1 can Cream of Potato soup
1/2 cup milk
6 eggs, lightly beaten

Sprinkle cheese in pie shell. Distribute chicken over top. Combine soup and milk until thoroughly mixed. Stir in eggs and pour into pie shell. Bake at 350° for 35 to 40 minutes or until golden and knife inserted into center comes out clean. Remove from oven and let stand 5 minutes before cutting. Makes 6 servings.

Lighter Version:
Lowfat Swiss cheese
Nonfat milk
Egg substitute

	Cal	Pro	Carb	Fib	Fat	Sat	Chol	Sod
Regular	368	20g	21g	1g	22g	8g	246mg	698mg
Lighter	304	21g	21g	1g	15g	4g	23mg	743mg

Company Chicken with Rice

A version of this wonderful casserole is included in most of my cookbooks. The recipe goes together in less than ten minutes and it makes a great family or company dish, is good reheated, is delicious, etc. (See why I use it a lot?) Enjoy!

OVEN 350°

6 chicken breast halves
1¹/₂ cups uncooked long-grain rice
1 can Broccoli Cheese soup
1 can Cream of Chicken soup
1 can Cream of Mushroom soup
¹/₂ cup slivered almonds

Clean chicken and pat dry. Distribute rice in 13x9-inch baking dish sprayed with nonstick cooking spray. In medium mixing bowl, combine the three soups. Gradually stir in 1¹/₂ soup cans water and blend until smooth. Add almonds. Carefully pour over rice. Stir to make sure rice grains are coated well with the sauce. Place chicken, skin-side up, in dish. Bake, uncovered, at 350° for 1¹/₂ hours or until liquid is absorbed and rice is tender. Makes 6 servings.

TIP: I prefer using chicken breasts with the bone in and skin left on. This prevents the chicken from drying out because of the long cooking time.

Lighter Version:
"Healthy Request" soups
Remove skin from chicken before eating
Omit almonds

	Cal	Pro	Carb	Fib	Fat	Sat	Chol	Sod
Regular	590	39g	54g	3g	24g	6g	91mg	1242mg
Lighter	437	34g	52g	2g	9g	3g	86mg	833mg

Garlic Chicken Casserole

A good standby recipe for almost any occasion. Bake and serve in an attractive baking dish or small roasting pan. This may seem like a lot of garlic, but baked garlic is really very mild.

Oven 400°

8 chicken pieces (4 legs, 4 thighs)
4 medium potatoes, peeled and quartered
8 large garlic cloves, unpeeled (see TIP)
Salt and pepper
1/4 cup butter, melted
1/4 cup honey

Place chicken, skin-side up, in 13x9-inch baking dish or roasting pan. Arrange potatoes and garlic around chicken. Sprinkle with salt and pepper. Pour butter over all. Bake at 400° for 40 minutes, basting once or twice with the pan juices. Drizzle honey over chicken. Bake 20 minutes or until chicken and vegetables are tender. Baste with pan juices and serve. Makes 4 servings.

TIP: Remove the thin paper-like skin on the garlic cloves, but do not peel.

Lighter Version:
4 chicken breast halves
Remove skin before eating
2 tablespoons butter

	Cal	Pro	Carb	Fib	Fat	Sat	Chol	Sod
Regular	544	32g	44g	2g	27g	11g	136mg	356mg
Lighter	370	29g	44g	2g	9g	4g	89mg	262mg

Italian Chicken Casserole

You can put this casserole together in about 10 minutes.
The aroma from the oven is heavenly.

Top Of Stove
OVEN 350°

4 chicken breast halves
1 cup uncooked long-grain rice
1 (0.7 ounce) package Italian salad dressing mix
1 can Cream of Chicken soup
1/2 cup slivered almonds
Salt and pepper

Clean chicken and pat dry with paper towels. Place rice in nonstick skillet (no oil) and cook over medium-low heat, stirring frequently, until most of the grains are light golden in color (watch carefully). Place rice in 13x9-inch baking dish sprayed with nonstick cooking spray. In mixing bowl, slowly add 2¹/₂ cups water to soup and stir to blend. Add salad dressing mix and almonds. Pour over rice. Stir mixture to evenly distribute the rice. Arrange chicken, skin-side up, over top. Sprinkle lightly with salt and pepper. Cover with foil and bake at 350° for 60 minutes. Remove foil, baste chicken with some of the liquid and bake at 350° 30 to 40 minutes or until liquid is absorbed and rice is tender. Makes 4 servings.

TIP: To expand recipe, use 6 chicken breasts. If you forget to thaw the chicken, that's okay as long as the chicken was cleaned before freezing. Just place frozen pieces on top of rice.

Lighter Version:
"Healthy Request" soup
1/4 cup almonds

	Cal	Pro	Carb	Fib	Fat	Sat	Chol	Sod
Regular	549	38g	49g	3g	21g	4g	88mg	821mg
Lighter	428	33g	49g	2g	9g	2g	79mg	515mg

Spanish Rice with Chicken

A good family-type recipe. Also low in fat.

Top Of Stove
Oven 350°

4 chicken breast halves
2 tablespoons oil
1/2 cup chopped onion
1 cup uncooked long-grain rice
1 (14 1/2-ounce) can stewed tomatoes
Salt and pepper, to taste

Brown chicken in heated oil, but do not cook. Remove chicken from skillet and set aside. Add onion and cook until soft. Remove onion and set aside. Pour juice from tomatoes into a large measuring cup. Add water to measure 2 1/2 cups. Add salt and pepper to taste. Sprinkle rice in 11x7-inch baking dish sprayed with nonstick cooking spray. Top with tomatoes (chopped, if pieces are large) and onion. Add tomato juice. Arrange chicken, skin-side up, in baking dish. Cover with foil and bake at 350° for 45 minutes. Remove foil and bake 20 to 30 minutes or until liquid is absorbed and rice is tender. Makes 4 servings.

TIP: This recipe seems to need a little more salt than you would think. You can add additional salt during the cooking stage or serve and let everyone add salt, as desired.

<u>Lighter Version:</u>
Omit oil
Brown chicken in nonstick skillet sprayed with cooking spray
Remove skin from chicken before eating

	Cal	Pro	Carb	Fib	Fat	Sat	Chol	Sod
Regular	467	34g	46g	2g	15g	3g	82mg	239mg
Lighter	356	32g	46g	2g	4g	1g	73mg	233mg

Wild Rice Chicken Casserole

If you don't tell anyone, they will never know there is only half a chicken breast in the entire recipe. Add a nice tossed green salad or a fruit salad and hot buttered French rolls. A good busy day casserole.

Top Of Stove
Oven 350°

1 chicken breast half, cooked and cubed, about 1 cup
1 (6-ounce) package Long-Grain and Wild Rice mix
1 can Cream of Mushroom soup
1 (5-ounce) can sliced water chestnuts, drained
1 cup finely chopped onion
1 cup finely chopped celery

If chicken isn't already cooked, you can microwave it, steam it, or place in a small skillet with about an inch of water. Cook, turning once, until cooked through. Let cool slightly, then cube. Meanwhile, cook rice according to package directions, but omit the butter and salt. Add chicken and remaining ingredients to the cooked rice; mix thoroughly. Pour into 8x8-inch baking dish sprayed with nonstick cooking spray. Cover with foil and bake at 350° for 30 minutes. Remove foil and bake 20 to 30 minutes or until liquid is absorbed. Makes 6 servings.

VARIATION: Increase chicken to 2 cups, omit onion and add 1 cup mayonnaise.

Lighter Version:
"Healthy Request" soup

	Cal	Pro	Carb	Fib	Fat	Sat	Chol	Sod
Regular	215	9g	34g	2g	5g	1g	13mg	444mg
Lighter	192	9g	34g	2g	2g	1g	16mg	232mg

Family Chicken Dinner

This casserole goes together surprisingly fast. Add a green vegetable, fruit salad and rolls for a complete meal.

Top Of Stove
Oven 350°

1 chicken, cut up
1/3 cup flour
Salt and pepper
2 tablespoons oil
1 1/2 cups uncooked long-grain rice
1 cup milk

Wash chicken pieces and pat dry. Season flour with a little salt and pepper. Coat chicken with the flour and brown in heated oil in medium skillet (do not cook through). Meanwhile, place rice in 13x9-inch baking dish sprayed with nonstick cooking spray. Add milk, salt and pepper to taste and 2 1/3 cups water; stir to coat and evenly distribute rice in dish. Place chicken over top, cover with foil and bake at 350° for 50 minutes. Uncover; bake 5 to 10 minutes or until chicken is tender and liquid is absorbed. Makes 4 servings.

TIP: The rice has a very mild flavor, which is rather nice for a change, and kids love it. But, if more flavor is desired, you could add some mixed herbs, chicken broth for the water and 1 teaspoon grated orange peel.

Lighter Version:
4 chicken breast halves
Omit oil and brown chicken in nonstick skillet sprayed with cooking spray
Nonfat milk
Remove skin from chicken before eating

	Cal	Pro	Carb	Fib	Fat	Sat	Chol	Sod
Regular	764	50g	71g	2g	29g	7g	136mg	209mg
Lighter	479	36g	71g	2g	4g	1g	74mg	151mg

Baked Chicken Sandwich

Makes a wonderful lunch or light supper dish. Serve with soup and a relish tray or salad and a fresh fruit cup.

OVEN 350°

4 ounces cream cheese, softened ($^1/_2$ of an 8-ounce package)
2 tablespoons butter, softened
1 cup cubed cooked chicken
$^1/_4$ cup chopped green onion (green part)
1 (8-ounce) package refrigerated Crescent rolls
$^1/_2$ cup (2-ounces) Cheddar cheese, shredded

Combine cream cheese and butter in a small mixer bowl and beat until smooth. By hand, stir in the chicken and green onion. Separate Crescent rolls into 8 triangles. Divide cream cheese mixture into 8 portions. Spread each portion on a triangle and roll up. Place in 8x8-inch baking dish sprayed with nonstick cooking spray. Sprinkle with cheese. Bake at 350° for 15 to 20 minutes or until lightly browned. Makes 4 servings.

TIP: Don't omit the green onion - it adds a lot of flavor as well as color.

Lighter Version:
Nonfat cream cheese (brick type)
Lowfat Cheddar cheese

	Cal	Pro	Carb	Fib	Fat	Sat	Chol	Sod
Regular	309	15g	8g	0g	25g	14g	86mg	379mg
Lighter	202	17g	8g	0g	11g	6g	48mg	380mg

Chicken in a Dish

Serve with a salad and delicious muffins hot from the oven.

4/28/02

Top Of Stove
Oven 350°

4 chicken breast halves, skinned and boned
4 tablespoons butter, divided
3¹/2 cups hot cooked rice
¹/2 cup slivered almonds
1¹/2 cups (6-ounces) Monterey Jack cheese, shredded
1 teaspoon dried parsley

Heat 2 tablespoons of the butter in a large skillet. Add chicken and lightly brown on both sides. (You want to brown the chicken, but not cook it.) Toss rice with remaining butter. Spread in 11x7-inch baking dish sprayed with nonstick cooking spray. Sprinkle almonds over rice. Sprinkle with cheese and then the parsley. Arrange chicken over top. Bake at 350° for 40 to 45 minutes until heated through and chicken is tender. Makes 4 servings.

<u>Lighter Version:</u>
Omit first 2 tablespoons butter
Brown chicken in nonstick skillet sprayed with cooking spray
Lowfat Monterey Jack cheese

	Cal	Pro	Carb	Fib	Fat	Sat	Chol	Sod
Regular	735	45g	54g	3g	37g	17g	142mg	413mg
Lighter	596	47g	52g	2g	21g	10g	119mg	995mg

Easy Baked Chicken

A super dish that all family members will enjoy. The vegetables add a lot of color and the sauce is great served over rice or noodles.

Oven 350°

6 small chicken breast halves, skinned and boned
¼ cup butter
6 small fresh broccoli spears
1 (5-ounce) can sliced water chestnuts, drained
2 small red pepper, cut into rings
1 can Cream of Chicken soup

Tuck ends of chicken breast underneath forming a nice mound or bundle. Place in 11x7-inch baking dish. Cut butter into small pieces and place over chicken. Bake 20 minutes. While chicken is baking, steam broccoli over a small amount of water until it turns bright green, but no longer. Remove chicken from oven and baste with butter. Place broccoli around chicken. Top with water chestnuts and pepper rings. Stir soup until smooth. Pour over chicken. Return to oven and bake 20 to 25 minutes or until chicken is cooked through. Makes 6 servings.

TIP: For 4 servings, reduce amount of chicken but use remaining ingredients.

Lighter Version:
2 tablespoons butter
"Healthy Request" soup

	Cal	Pro	Carb	Fib	Fat	Sat	Chol	Sod
Regular	281	29g	9g	2g	14g	7g	98mg	550mg
Lighter	234	29g	10g	2g	8g	4g	88mg	316mg

Chicken Divan

A cookbook wouldn't be complete without a "Divan" recipe.

4 chicken breast halves, skinned and boned
8 small fresh broccoli spears (2 per serving)
1 cup mayonnaise
2 teaspoons prepared mustard
¼ cup finely chopped onion
1 cup (4-ounces) Cheddar cheese, shredded

Steam chicken, or cover with water and cook until chicken tests done. Meanwhile, steam broccoli until just crisp-tender. Place broccoli in a 8x8-inch baking dish sprayed with nonstick cooking spray. Slice each chicken breast lengthwise into three slices; place over and around broccoli. Combine mayonnaise, mustard and onion; spread over chicken. Top with cheese. Bake at 350° for 30 minutes or until heated through. Makes 4 servings.

TIP: Leftover chicken or turkey slices may be used as well as a 10-ounce package of frozen broccoli spears.

Lighter Version:
3 chicken breast halves
Light mayonnaise
Lowfat Cheddar cheese

	Cal	Pro	Carb	Fib	Fat	Sat	Chol	Sod
Regular	709	41g	12g	6g	57g	13g	136mg	629mg
Lighter	357	33g	21g	6g	17g	4g	76mg	441mg

Chicken Divan with Cream Cheese

A wonderfully delicious one-dish meal.

4 chicken breast halves, skinned and boned
2 tablespoons oil
1 (8-ounce) package cream cheese
1 cup milk
³/4 cup freshly grated Parmesan cheese, divided
8 small fresh broccoli spears

Cook chicken in heated oil until lightly browned and cooked almost through. If chicken is cooked too long, it may be tough and dry after baking. Place chicken in 11x7-inch baking dish sprayed with nonstick cooking spray. While chicken is cooking, place cream cheese and milk in top of double boiler. Cook over low heat until cream cheese is melted and mixture is blended. Stir in ¹/2 cup of the Parmesan cheese. Meanwhile, steam broccoli until it turns a bright green (do not cook any longer). Place around chicken. Pour cream cheese mixture over top. Sprinkle with remaining ¹/4 cup Parmesan cheese. Bake at 350° for 30 minutes.

TIP: If chicken breasts are quite large, I would suggest cutting them in half.

Lighter Version:
Omit oil and use skillet sprayed with nonstick cooking spray
Light cream cheese
Nonfat milk
¹/2 cup Parmesan cheese

	Cal	Pro	Carb	Fib	Fat	Sat	Chol	Sod
Regular	617	52g	23g	11g	38g	18g	155mg	705mg
Lighter	452	51g	26g	11g	18g	10g	116mg	589mg

Busy Day Chicken

This easy to make casserole is delicious anytime.

4 chicken breast halves, skinned and boned
1¼ pounds fresh asparagus spears, trimmed
1 can Cream of Chicken soup
1 cup Half and Half
¹/₃ cup freshly grated Parmesan cheese
¹/₄ cup sliced almonds

Lightly brown chicken in a nonstick skillet sprayed with cooking spray. While chicken is cooking, remove tough ends from asparagus and rinse. Spray 11x7-inch baking dish with nonstick cooking spray; lay asparagus in dish with tips towards the center. Heat soup and Half and Half in medium saucepan. Reduce heat and gradually add Parmesan cheese until melted. Place chicken over asparagus and pour sauce over top. Sprinkle with almonds. Cover with foil and bake at 350° for 45 to 50 minutes or until chicken is tender. Makes 4 servings.

Lighter Version:
"Healthy Request" soup
Nonfat milk
¹/₄ cup Parmesan cheese
2 tablespoons almonds

	Cal	Pro	Carb	Fib	Fat	Sat	Chol	Sod
Regular	395	38g	16g	4g	20g	8g	108mg	844mg
Lighter	293	36g	17g	4g	8g	3g	85mg	522mg

Chicken Enchiladas in Cream

This recipe appears in my Chicken cookbook, but it bears repeating here.
It is a recipe that is great anytime; family, company, potluck . . .

Oven 350°

3 cups cubed cooked chicken
1 cup green chili salsa (actually red in color)
1 (4-ounce) can chopped green chilies
10 (8-inch) flour tortillas
2¹/₂ cups whipping cream
2 cups Monterey Jack cheese, shredded

Combine chicken, salsa and chilies in large mixing bowl. Fill each tortilla
with ¹/₁₀th of the mixture. Roll up and place, seam-side down, in 13x9-inch
baking dish sprayed with nonstick cooking spray. Pour cream over top.
Sprinkle evenly with cheese. Bake at 350° for 45 minutes or until golden
and most of the cream is absorbed. Makes 6 servings.

Lighter Version:
Lowfat tortillas
Half and Half
Lowfat Monterey Jack cheese

	Cal	Pro	Carb	Fib	Fat	Sat	Chol	Sod
Regular	780	35g	39g	2g	54g	31g	217mg	938mg
Lighter	460	37g	34g	7g	22g	12g	111mg	1218mg

Chicken and Green Bean Casserole

A super potluck casserole.

1 (6-ounce) package Long-Grain and Wild Rice mix
3 cups cubed cooked chicken
2 (14.5-ounce) cans French-style green beans, drained
1 can Cream of Mushroom soup
1 cup mayonnaise
1 (5-ounce) can sliced water chestnuts, drained

Cook rice according to package directions. Meanwhile, combine remaining ingredients in large mixing bowl. Add rice. Pour into a 2^1/$_2$ to 3-quart deep casserole dish sprayed with nonstick cooking spray. Bake at 350° for 60 minutes or until heated through. Makes 8 to 10 servings.

Lighter Version:
All white meat
"Healthy Request" soup
Light sour cream

	Cal	Pro	Carb	Fib	Fat	Sat	Chol	Sod
Regular	406	15g	29g	3g	26g	4g	44mg	758mg
Lighter	232	15g	29g	3g	6g	3g	42mg	458mg

Chicken and Broccoli Dish

*A quick and easy Chicken Divan type recipe. The sauce is
excellent served over rice.*

Top of Stove
Oven 350°

4 chicken breast halves, skinned and boned
4 serving size pieces of fresh broccoli with stems
1 can Cream of Chicken soup
1 cup mayonnaise
1/4 cup sherry
1/2 cup freshly grated Parmesan cheese, divided

Quickly brown chicken breasts in a nonstick skillet sprayed with cooking
spray. Place rounded side up in 8x8-inch baking dish sprayed with nonstick cooking spray. Microwave or steam broccoli until it turns a bright
green (this shouldn't take more than 2 to 3 minutes). Place broccoli around
chicken. Combine soup, mayonnaise, sherry and 1/4 cup of the Parmesan
cheese, blending until smooth. Pour over chicken. Sprinkle with remaining 1/4 cup Parmesan cheese. Bake at 350° for 30 minutes or until chicken is
cooked through. Makes 4 servings.

TIP: If this casserole is too salty for your taste buds, decrease the amount of
Parmesan cheese used.

Lighter Version:
Substitute nonfat yogurt for mayonnaise
1/4 cup Parmesan cheese
"Healthy Request" soup

	Cal	Pro	Carb	Fib	Fat	Sat	Chol	Sod
Regular	708	37g	13g	2g	56g	11g	122mg	1231mg
Lighter	298	36g	17g	3g	7g	3g	85mg	549mg

Chicken Mushroom Casserole

The water chestnuts add an extra crunch to this popular casserole. Serve the sauce over rice or noodles.

Oven 350°

1 chicken, cut up
1/4 cup butter
8 ounces fresh mushrooms, quartered
1 (5-ounce) can sliced water chestnuts, drained
1 can Cream of Chicken soup
2 tablespoons chopped parsley (or 1 tablespoon dried)

Place chicken, skin-side down, in 13x9-inch baking dish. Dot with butter. Bake at 350° for 20 minutes. Turn chicken; bake for 20 minutes. Add mushrooms and water chestnuts to dish. Stir soup; spoon over chicken. Sprinkle with parsley. Bake 20 minutes or until chicken is cooked through. Makes 4 servings.

TIP: If your oven cooks a little slow, I would increase the temperature to 375° or bake about 10 to 15 minutes longer.

Lighter Version:
Chicken breast halves
Remove skin from chicken before eating
2 tablespoons butter
"Healthy Request" soup

	Cal	Pro	Carb	Fib	Fat	Sat	Chol	Sod
Regular	559	44g	12g	2g	36g	14g	169mg	844mg
Lighter	274	29g	14g	2g	11g	5g	95mg	434mg

Chicken Fajita Casserole

I don't always have time to make Fajitas from scratch, but Tyson has come to the rescue. They have a frozen Fajita Chicken meat that is seasoned and cooked chicken. It is convenient to use when you are in a hurry and makes a very good casserole such as the one below.

TOP OF STOVE
OVEN 350°

4 cups frozen Chicken Fajita meat
1 medium onion, halved, cut into wedges
2 small peppers (1 red and 1 green)
8 (8-inch) flour tortillas
1¹/₂ cups (6-ounces) Cheddar cheese, shredded
1¹/₂ cups salsa

Place chicken pieces in a large skillet and add 2 tablespoons water. Cook over medium heat until chicken is thawed and heated through. Add onion and peppers. Cover and cook 4 to 5 minutes or until vegetables are tender but still crisp.

Place a portion of the mixture in the center of a tortilla. Sprinkle with a little of the cheese and roll up. Place in 13x9-inch baking dish sprayed with nonstick cooking spray. Sprinkle with remaining cheese. Bake at 325° just until heated through and cheese is melted. Serve topped with salsa. Makes 4 servings.

Lighter Version:
Lowfat Cheddar cheese
Make 8 servings instead of 4

	Cal	Pro	Carb	Fib	Fat	Sat	Chol	Sod
Regular	679	46g	52g	4g	32g	14g	195mg	1875mg
Lighter	291	23g	26g	2g	11g	3g	80mg	810mg

Chicken Noodle Casserole

Serve this delicious casserole with a nice tossed green salad, a side dish of broccoli and a loaf of crusty bread.

Top Of Stove
Oven 350°

6 ounces fettuccine noodles
1 can Cream of Mushroom soup
1 1/2 cups (6-ounces) Cheddar cheese, shredded, divided
2/3 cup milk
2 cups cooked cubed chicken
1/4 cup slivered or sliced almonds

Cook fettuccine according to package directions; drain. Meanwhile, place the soup, 1 cup of the cheese and milk in a medium saucepan. Heat until cheese is melted, stirring to blend. Spread a thin layer of sauce over bottom of an 11x7-inch baking dish sprayed with nonstick cooking spray. Arrange half the noodles on top.

Add chicken to remaining sauce. Pour half the sauce over noodles. Layer with remaining noodles and pour remaining sauce over top. Sprinkle with remaining 1/2 cup cheese. Srinkle with almonds. Bake at 350° for 60 minutes. Let stand 5 to 10 minutes before serving. Makes 6 servings.

Lighter Version:
"Healthy Request" soup
Lowfat Cheddar cheese
Nonfat milk
2 tablespoons almonds

	Cal	Pro	Carb	Fib	Fat	Sat	Chol	Sod
Regular	385	27g	29g	2g	18g	8g	69mg	632mg
Lighter	282	27g	28g	2g	6g	2g	47mg	255mg

Sour Cream Noodle Bake

*We can never have too many ground beef casseroles. This is also a good
way to use up that last cup of sour cream and cottage cheese.*

Top Of Stove
O<small>VEN</small> 350°

6 ounces egg noodles
1 pound lean ground beef
1 (28-ounce) jar chunky spaghetti sauce with mushrooms
1 cup sour cream
1 cup small curd cottage cheese
1 cup (4-ounces) Cheddar cheese, shredded

Cook noodles according to package directions; drain. Meanwhile, brown
ground beef; drain off fat. Add spaghetti sauce and cook over medium low
heat, about 15 minutes or until some of the liquid is absorbed. Combine
noodles with sour cream and cottage cheese, mixing well to blend. Pour
into 11x7-inch baking dish sprayed with nonstick cooking spray. Spread
meat sauce over top. Sprinkle with cheese. Bake at 350° for 30 minutes.
Makes 6 servings.

Lighter Version:
3/4 pound ground chicken
Light sour cream
Nonfat cottage cheese
3 ounces lowfat Cheddar cheese

	Cal	Pro	Carb	Fib	Fat	Sat	Chol	Sod
Regular	536	31g	34g	4g	31g	15g	116mg	1016mg
Lighter	400	27g	34g	4g	17g	6g	80mg	908mg

Linda's Beef Curry Casserole

*My daughter, Linda, is a wonderful cook and her Beef Curry
Casserole has become a family favorite.*

Top Of Stove
Oven 350°

1 pound lean ground beef
3/4 cup uncooked long-grain rice
1 1/2 teaspoons salt
1 1/2 teaspoons curry powder (or to taste)
1 (8-ounce) can crushed pineapple, with juice
1/2 cup raisins

Cook rice according to package directions, except omit the butter and salt.
Meanwhile, brown ground beef in large skillet; drain off fat. Add salt and
curry to meat. Stir in pineapple and raisins. Bring to a boil, reduce heat and
simmer 3 to 4 minutes. Add rice and place mixture in a 2-quart deep casserole
dish sprayed with nonstick cooking spray. Bake, covered, at 350° for 30
minutes to heat through and blend flavors. Makes 6 servings.

Lighter Version:
3/4 pound ground chicken

	Cal	Pro	Carb	Fib	Fat	Sat	Chol	Sod
Regular	304	18g	36g	1g	10g	4g	51mg	572mg
Lighter	255	14g	36g	1g	6g	1g	37mg	572mg

Pasta Shell Tacos

It's amazing what you can do with ground beef and pasta.
Kids love this simple casserole dish.

Top Of Stove

14 jumbo pasta shells
1 pound lean ground beef
1 package taco seasoning mix
1 cup (4-ounces) Cheddar cheese, shredded
Salsa
Sour cream

Cook pasta shells according to package directions; drain well and rinse with cold water. Meanwhile, brown ground beef in skillet; drain off fat. Add taco seasoning mix and water as directed on package. Simmer over low heat for 15 to 20 minutes. Fill shells with meat mixture and place in baking dish sprayed with nonstick cooking spray (I like to use my 10-inch deep pie dish for this recipe - the pasta shells seem to stand up better against the round edges). Sprinkle cheese over top. Bake at 350° for 10 to 15 minutes to heat through and melt the cheese. Serve topped with salsa and a dollop of sour cream. Makes about 4 servings.

TIP: If desired, substitute about 1/2 cup salsa for the taco seasoning mix. Serve with additional salsa and sour cream. Also good with chopped tomato and shredded lettuce.

Lighter Version:
1 pound ground chicken
Lowfat Cheddar cheese
Omit sour cream

	Cal	Pro	Carb	Fib	Fat	Sat	Chol	Sod
Regular	513	35g	30g	2g	27g	13g	113mg	658mg
Lighter	396	36g	29g	2g	13g	4g	79mg	498mg

Soft Taco Casserole

A hearty meat dish that's sure to please the men around the house.

Top Of Stove
Oven 350°

1¹/₂ pounds lean ground beef
1 package taco seasoning mix
5 (8-inch) flour tortillas (if necessary, trim to fit dish)
2 cups (8-ounces) medium Cheddar cheese, shredded
1 (16-ounce) can refried beans
1 cup salsa

Brown ground beef in large skillet; drain off fat. Add taco seasoning and 1 cup water. Cook over low heat, about 10 minutes, to blend flavors and cook off most of the liquid. Meat should still be quite moist. In 8x8-inch baking dish sprayed with nonstick cooking spray, layer half of the ground beef, 1 tortilla, half of the cheese, 1 tortilla, half of the beans, 1 tortilla. Then layer remaining ground beef, 1 tortilla, remaining beans, 1 tortilla and remaining cheese. Spread salsa over top. Bake at 350° for 35 to 40 minutes or until heated through. Makes 6 generous servings.

Lighter Version:
Lowfat Cheddar cheese
Lowfat refried beans
Lowfat tortillas

	Cal	Pro	Carb	Fib	Fat	Sat	Chol	Sod
Regular	582	40g	37g	5g	30g	14g	116mg	1147mg
Lighter	356	31g	31g	8g	13g	6g	59mg	959mg

Pot Luck Casserole

*This filling dish packs an impressive amount of flavor with little effort
and time spent in the kitchen.*

Top Of Stove
Oven 350°

2 pounds lean ground beef
2 cups coarsely chopped onion
1 (30-ounce) jar extra chunky spaghetti sauce (3 cups)
8 ounces (about 2¹/₂ cups uncooked) small shell macaroni
1¹/₂ cups sour cream
1 (16-ounce) package Mozzarella cheese, shredded

In large skillet, brown ground beef and onion; pour off fat. Stir in spaghetti sauce. Cook over low heat about 8 to 10 minutes to reduce some of the liquid. Meanwhile, cook shells according to package directions, undercooking just slightly. In 13x9-inch baking dish sprayed with non-stick cooking spray, layer half of the cooked shells, half of the meat mixture, half of the sour cream and half the cheese. Repeat with remaining ingredients. Bake at 350° for 30 to 35 minutes or until heated through and cheese is golden. Makes 8 to 10 servings.

TIP: Dish will be quite full. Baking dish should be at least 2-inches deep.

Lighter Version:
1¹/₂ pounds ground chicken
Light sour cream
12 ounces light Mozzarella cheese

	Cal	Pro	Carb	Fib	Fat	Sat	Chol	Sod
Regular	682	46g	41g	4g	37g	18g	126mg	938mg
Lighter	590	43g	40g	4g	28g	11g	114mg	875mg

Picnic Hamburger and Beans

A quick and tasty dish for your next picnic or potluck.

1½ pounds lean ground beef
2 cups chopped onion
1 (3 pound, 5-ounce) can pork and beans
1 (14½-ounce) can whole tomatoes, drained
½ cup firmly packed light brown sugar
½ cup ketchup

Brown ground beef and onion in very large skillet or pot; drain off fat. Add beans. Cut up the tomatoes and add. Stir in brown sugar and ketchup and cook until heated through. Pour into a 3-quart deep casserole dish sprayed with nonstick cooking spray. Bake at 350° for 50 to 60 minutes. Makes 10 servings.

TIP: If more juice is desired in casserole, bake 50 minutes. For a thicker casserole, bake 60 minutes. Mixture will also thicken somewhat as it stands.

<u>Lighter Version:</u>
1 pound ground chicken

	Cal	Pro	Carb	Fib	Fat	Sat	Chol	Sod
Regular	342	22g	44g	8g	10g	4g	56mg	905mg
Lighter	288	18g	44g	8g	6g	2g	40mg	901mg

Taco Rice Dish

Delicious served with sour cream and tortilla chips.

Top Of Stove
Oven 350°

1 cup uncooked long-grain rice
1 pound lean ground beef
1 cup chopped onion
1½ cups chunky salsa
1 (8-ounce) can tomato sauce
1 cup (4-ounces) Cheddar cheese, shredded

Cook rice according to package directions, but omit the salt and butter. Meanwhile, in large skillet, brown ground beef and onion; drain off fat. Stir in salsa and tomato sauce. Bring to a boil, reduce heat, and simmer while rice is cooking or for about 10 minutes. Spread rice in 11x7-inch baking dish sprayed with nonstick cooking spray. Top with meat sauce and sprinkle with cheese. Bake at 350° for 15 minutes to melt cheese. Makes 6 servings.

VARIATION: Add sliced ripe olives to meat sauce.

Lighter Version:
1 pound ground chicken
Lowfat Cheddar cheese

	Cal	Pro	Carb	Fib	Fat	Sat	Chol	Sod
Regular	383	24g	35g	2g	16g	8g	71mg	618mg
Lighter	326	24g	35g	2g	9g	3g	53mg	516mg

Chili Oven Casserole

A popular dish when boating or camping. You can make it at home and reheat on your first night out. And it feeds an army -- well, a small army.

Top Of Stove
Oven 350°

2 pounds lean ground beef
1¼ cups chopped onion
2 medium tomatoes, diced
1 medium green pepper, diced (about ¾ cup)
2 (15-ounce) cans chili with beans

Brown ground beef and onion in a large pot or deep skillet; drain off fat. Stir in remaining ingredients. Pour in 2¾-quart deep casserole sprayed with nonstick cooking spray. Cover and bake at 350° for 60 minutes. Makes 8 servings.

Lighter Version
1½ pounds ground chicken
Lowfat chili with beans

	Cal	Pro	Carb	Fib	Fat	Sat	Chol	Sod
Regular	363	29g	17g	6g	20g	8g	94mg	613mg
Lighter	262	26g	15g	3g	10g	3g	69mg	569mg

Lasagna Casserole

*Slightly faster than layering; just toss together the
cooked ingredients and bake.*

Top Of Stove
Oven 350°

1 (20-ounce) package cut lasagna noodles
1 pound lean ground beef
8 ounces fresh mushrooms, sliced
1/2 cup sliced ripe olives
4 1/2 cups chunky-type spaghetti sauce
2 cups (8-ounces) Mozzarella cheese, shredded

Cook pasta according to package directions; drain and rinse with cold water. Meanwhile, cook ground beef in large skillet until just pink. Add mushrooms and cook, stirring frequently, until meat is cooked through; drain off fat Add olives and spaghetti sauce. Bring to a boil, reduce heat and simmer 10 to 15 minutes to slightly reduce liquid and blend flavors. Place pasta in 13x9-inch baking dish sprayed with nonstick cooking spray. Pour meat sauce over top and gently stir to coat the pasta. Sprinkle with cheese. Bake at 350° for 30 minutes or until heated through and cheese is lightly browned. Makes 8 servings.

TIP: Ruffle-edged noodles average about 1 1/2 to 2 inches in length.

Lighter Version:
3/4 pound ground chicken
Light Mozarrella cheese

	Cal	Pro	Carb	Fib	Fat	Sat	Chol	Sod
Regular	556	30g	65g	6g	20g	7g	53mg	1041mg
Lighter	520	28g	65g	6g	17g	5g	43mg	1041mg

Hamburger Rice Casserole

*Good ground beef recipes are hard to find and this one is hearty
enough for even the hungriest of appetites.*

Top Of Stove
Oven 350°

1 pound lean ground beef
3/4 cup chopped onion
1 1/2 cups uncooked long-grain rice
1/2 cup toasted slivered almonds
1 can Cream of Celery soup
1 can Cream of Mushroom soup

Brown ground beef and onion in a medium skillet; drain off fat. Stir in rice
and almonds; pour into 11x7-inch baking dish sprayed with nonstick cooking spray. In mixing bowl, combine the soups. Gradually stir in 2 1/2 cups
water, stirring until smooth. Pour over meat mixture (dish will be quite
full). Bake at 350° for 60 minutes or until liquid is absorbed and rice is
tender. Makes 6 servings.

Lighter Version:
3/4 pound ground chicken
1/4 cup almonds
"Healthy Request" soup

	Cal	Pro	Carb	Fib	Fat	Sat	Chol	Sod
Regular	499	23g	51g	3g	22g	6g	57mg	836mg
Lighter	387	19g	51g	2g	11g	2g	42mg	439mg

Hamburger Cornbread Bake

A pound of ground beef goes a long way, the salsa adds a lot of flavor and the cornbread adds a nice crunch.

1 pound lean ground beef
1 cup whole corn (frozen or canned)
1¹/₂ cups salsa
1 (8¹/₂-ounce) package cornbread mix
¹/₃ cup milk
1 egg

Brown ground beef in a large skillet; drain off fat. Stir in corn and salsa. Bring to a boil, reduce heat, and simmer about 20 minutes or until liquid is absorbed. Pour into a 11x7-inch baking dish spayed with nonstick cooking spray. Follow directions on package for mixing corn bread. Spread evenly over meat mixture. Bake at 400° for 15 to 20 minutes or until golden brown. Makes 6 servings.

Lighter Version:
³/₄ pound ground chicken
Nonfat milk
Egg substitute

	Cal	Pro	Carb	Fib	Fat	Sat	Chol	Sod
Regular	371	21g	37g	3g	16g	5g	87mg	735mg
Lighter	317	18g	37g	3g	11g	3g	37mg	742mg

Chili Cornbread Dinner

An inexpensive family-type dish. Also good reheated.

3 (15-ounce) cans chili with beans
6 hot dogs
1 (8¹/₂-ounce) box cornbread mix
1 egg
¹/₃ cup milk

Place chili in medium saucepan and heat through. Pour into 11x7-inch baking dish sprayed with nonstick cooking spray. Cut hot dogs in half length-wise and place, cut side down, on chili. Combine cornbread mix, egg and milk and mix according to package directions. Carefully spread over meat mixture. Bake at 450° for 15 minutes or until cornbread is golden brown. Makes 6 servings.

VARIATION: Add one 11-ounce can Mexicorn, drained.

Lighter Version:
Lowfat chili
Turkey frankfurters
Egg substitute
Nonfat milk

	Cal	Pro	Carb	Fib	Fat	Sat	Chol	Sod
Regular	607	23g	55g	11g	34g	13g	101mg	2211mg
Lighter	464	25g	51g	7g	18g	5g	76mg	2136mg

Beef Broccoli with Rice

A wonderful, but rather strong, broccoli and mushroom
flavor. Makes a lot, but can be reheated.

Top Of Stove
Oven 350°

1¹/₂ cups uncooked long-grain rice
1 pound lean ground beef
1 (20-ounce) package frozen broccoli pieces
2 cans Cream of Mushroom soup
1 cup mayonnaise
2 cups (8-ounces) Cheddar cheese, shredded, divided

Cook rice according to package directions, but omit the butter and salt.
Brown ground beef; drain off fat. Place frozen broccoli in colander and run
under hot water. Drain and place in 13x9-inch baking dish sprayed with
nonstick cooking spray. Top with the rice. Combine soup and mayonnaise;
add ground beef and one cup cheese. Spread over rice. Sprinkle with remaining cheese. Bake at 350° for 45 minutes. Makes 8 to 10 servings.

TIP: Pyrex makes a rather deep 13x9x2-inch 3-quart baking dish that is
perfect for this recipe as well as others in the cookbook.

Lighter Version:
³/₄ pound ground chicken
"Healthy Request" soup
Light mayonnaise
Lowfat Cheddar cheese

	Cal	Pro	Carb	Fib	Fat	Sat	Chol	Sod
Regular	660	25g	40g	3g	45g	14g	85mg	994mg
Lighter	399	22g	45g	3g	14g	4g	47mg	511mg

Baked Spaghetti Casserole

A quick and easy spaghetti dish. Leftovers are wonderful reheated.

12 ounces spaghetti
1 pound lean ground beef
2 cups chunky spaghetti sauce
1¹/₂ cups (6-ounces) Cheddar cheese, shredded
1¹/₂ cups (6-ounces) Provolone cheese, shredded

Cook spaghetti according to package directions; drain. Meanwhile, brown ground beef in large skillet (no oil needed). Drain off fat. Add spaghetti sauce and heat through. Add noodles to meat mixture; toss to coat. Place half of the mixture in an 11x7-inch baking dish sprayed with nonstick cooking spray. Top with half the Cheddar and half the Provolone cheese. Repeat layers. Bake at 350° for 20 to 25 minutes or until heated through and cheese is golden. Makes 8 servings.

VARIATION: For variety, add olives, mushrooms, Parmesan cheese or zucchini.

<u>Lighter Version:</u>
³/₄ pound ground chicken
Lowfat Cheddar cheese
Lowfat Monterey Jack cheese

	Cal	Pro	Carb	Fib	Fat	Sat	Chol	Sod
Regular	486	29g	41g	3g	23g	11g	75mg	675mg
Lighter	355	24g	40g	3g	11g	4g	40mg	469mg

Tamale Casserole

If you like tamales, you will enjoy this casserole. A good family recipe.

Top Of Stove
Oven 350°

1 pound lean ground beef
1 cup chopped onion
1 (14¹/₂-ounce) can Thick & Chunky tomato sauce
2 tablespoons canned diced green chilies
8 (6-inch) corn tortillas
2 cups (8-ounces) Cheddar cheese, shredded

In large skillet, brown ground beef and onion; drain off fat. Add tomato sauce and green chilies. Tear 4 of the corn tortillas into bite-sized pieces and place in 11x7-inch dish sprayed with nonstick cooking spray. Add half the meat mixture, then half the cheese. Repeat layers ending with cheese. Bake at 350° for 25 to 30 minutes. Makes 6 servings.

Lighter Version:
1 pound ground chicken
Use lowfat cheddar cheese

	Cal	Pro	Carb	Fib	Fat	Sat	Chol	Sod
Regular	423	28g	27g	3g	23g	12g	91mg	784mg
Lighter	322	29g	27g	3g	11g	4g	57mg	569mg

Parmesan Noodles and Ham

A delicious and somewhat dry type of casserole. A nice change from our popular, and much loved, cream sauces.

Top Of Stove
Oven 350°

6 ounces rigatoni
4 to 5 green onions, sliced into 1-inch pieces
1 teaspoon oil
4 ounces (about 1 cup) small cubed ham
3 tablespoons slivered almonds
1/2 cup plus 2 tablespoons freshly grated Parmesan cheese

Cook noodles according to package directions. Toss onion with oil and cook in medium skillet until soft. Add ham and almonds; cook until heated through. Add drained noodles and the 1/2 cup Parmesan cheese. Pour into 1 1/2-quart deep casserole dish sprayed with nonstick cooking spray. Sprinkle with remaining 2 tablespoons cheese. Bake at 350° for about 15 minutes or until heated through. Makes 4 large servings.

TIP: To use as a side dish, omit ham and add 1/2 cup peas.

Lighter Version:
Canadian bacon
2 tablespoons almonds
1/4 cup plus 1 tablespoon Parmesan cheese

	Cal	Pro	Carb	Fib	Fat	Sat	Chol	Sod
Regular	322	19g	36g	3g	11g	4g	24mg	577mg
Lighter	285	16g	36g	2g	8g	3g	20mg	548mg

Ham Swiss Cheese Casserole

Nothing fancy here, but still flavorful and filling.

8 ounces ham
1 cup uncooked long-grain rice
2 tablespoons butter
3 eggs, lightly beaten
1¹/₃ cups milk
2 cups (8-ounces) Swiss cheese, shredded

Cut ham into small cubes, set aside. Cook rice according to package directions, but omit the butter and salt. Remove from heat and gently stir in butter, then the ham. Combine eggs and milk, mixing with a whisk to blend. Add to rice mixture along with the cheese. Pour into 11x7-inch baking dish sprayed with nonstick cooking spray. Bake at 350° for 45 to 50 minutes or until set. Makes 6 servings.

TIP: Can reheat.

Lighter Version:
Canadian bacon
1 tablespoon butter
Egg substitute
Nonfat milk
Lowfat Swiss cheese

	Cal	Pro	Carb	Fib	Fat	Sat	Chol	Sod
Regular	408	25g	31g	1g	20g	11g	171mg	572mg
Lighter	298	25g	31g	1g	7g	3g	34mg	602mg

Ham and Rotini Casserole

A little bit of ham goes a long way in this family-type casserole.

16 ounces rotini
1/2 cup butter, divided
3 tablespoons flour
1 1/3 cups milk
1/2 pound ham, cubed
3/4 cup freshly grated Parmesan cheese, divided

Cook pasta according to package directions; drain, rinse and return to pot. Meanwhile, melt 2 tablespoons of the butter in small saucepan. Stir in flour until smooth; cook about 1 minute, stirring frequently. Remove from heat; add milk and whisk until smooth. Cook over low heat until thickened, stirring frequently. Add the remaining butter and heat until melted. Add ham and 1/2 cup of the Parmesan cheese. Toss sauce with noodles. Pour into 11x7-inch baking dish sprayed with nonstick cooking spray. Sprinkle remaining Parmesan cheese over top. Bake at 350° for 20 to 30 minutes or until heated through. Makes 6 servings.

<u>Lighter Version:</u>
2 tablespoons plus 3 tablespoons butter
6 ounces Canadian bacon
Nonfat milk
1/3 cup plus 1 tablespoon Parmesan cheese

	Cal	Pro	Carb	Fib	Fat	Sat	Chol	Sod
Regular	547	22g	55g	2g	26g	14g	73mg	754mg
Lighter	437	19g	55g	2g	15g	8g	46mg	650mg

Ham and Rice Dish

A tasty way to combine rice, orange marmalade and ham.

Top Of Stove
Oven 350°

1 cup uncooked long-grain rice
1/4 cup butter
1/3 cup slivered almonds
2/3 cup orange marmalade
4 ounces (about 1 cup) cubed ham

Cook rice according to package directions, but omit the butter and salt. About five minutes before rice is done, melt butter in small skillet. Add almonds and lightly toast. Stir in marmalade and heat through. Spread half of the rice in a 2-quart deep casserole dish sprayed with nonstick cooking spray. Layer with half the ham and half the butter mixture. Repeat ending with the butter mixture. Cover and bake at 350° for 30 minutes. Remove cover and bake 5 minutes. Makes 4 servings.

Lighter Version:
2 tablespoons butter
4 ounces Canadian bacon

	Cal	Pro	Carb	Fib	Fat	Sat	Chol	Sod
Regular	501	11g	77g	2g	18g	8g	43mg	431mg
Lighter	462	12g	77g	2g	13g	5g	30mg	490mg

Green Bean Ham Casserole

A different version of a popular dish that has been around for a long time. I don't think anyone would guess there is only 4 ounces of ham in this casserole.

OVEN 350°

4 ounces (about 1 cup) cubed ham
2 (14.5-ounce) cans French-style green beans, drained
1 (5-ounce) can sliced water chestnuts, drained
1 can Cream of Mushroom soup
1 (2.25-ounce) can French-fried onion rings
1 cup (4-ounces) Cheddar cheese, shredded

Combine first four ingredients and pour into 11x7-inch baking dish sprayed with nonstick cooking spray. Bake at 350° for 20 minutes. Remove from oven and arrange onion rings over casserole. Sprinkle with cheese. Return to oven and bake 10 minutes. Makes 6 servings.

Lighter Version:
Canadian bacon
"Healthy Request" soup
Half the onion rings
Lowfat Cheddar cheese

	Cal	Pro	Carb	Fib	Fat	Sat	Chol	Sod
Regular	260	12g	21g	4g	15g	7g	29mg	1235mg
Lighter	214	11g	21g	4g	10g	3g	11mg	1036mg

Egg Casserole with Ham

*For an easy brunch or light supper, serve this delicious main dish with
assorted fresh fruit and hot-from-the-oven muffins.*

Oven 350°

1 cup (about 4-ounces) diced ham
¹/₄ cup sliced green onions (green and white part)
1 cup (4-ounces) Monterey Jack cheese, shredded
12 eggs, lightly beaten
2 cups Half and Half
¹/₈ teaspoon pepper

Sprinkle ham in 11x7-inch baking dish sprayed with nonstick cooking spray.
Add green onion. Top with shredded cheese. In large mixing bowl, com-
bine eggs, Half and Half and pepper; mix well to blend. Pour over cheese.
Bake at 350° for 40 to 45 minutes or until set. Makes 8 servings.

Lighter Version
Canadian bacon
Lowfat Monterey Jack cheese

	Cal	Pro	Carb	Fib	Fat	Sat	Chol	Sod
Regular	261	17g	4g	0g	19g	10g	359mg	334mg
Lighter	254	19g	4g	0g	18g	8g	357mg	426mg

Pork Chops and Rice Casserole

Always a company and family favorite.

Top Of Stove
Oven 350°

6 pork chops, ³/₄ to 1-inch thick
2 tablespoons oil
1¹/₂ cups uncooked long-grain rice
1 can Cream of Chicken soup
1 can Cream of Mushroom soup
1 can Cream of Celery soup

Trim fat from pork chops. Heat oil in large skillet. Add pork chops and quickly brown on both sides (do not cook). Place rice in 13x9-inch baking dish sprayed with nonstick cooking spray. Combine the three soups and gradually stir in 1¹/₂ soup cans water until blended. Pour over rice; stir to evenly distribute the rice. Arrange pork chops on top. Cover and bake at 350° for 60 minutes. Remove cover and bake 30 minutes or until liquid is absorbed and rice is tender. Makes 6 servings.

<u>Lighter Version:</u>
Omit oil
Brown meat in nonstick skillet sprayed with cooking spray
"Healthy Request" soups

	Cal	Pro	Carb	Fib	Fat	Sat	Chol	Sod
Regular	485	25g	51g	1g	19g	5g	62mg	1235mg
Lighter	400	24g	53g	1g	9g	3g	61mg	639mg

Pork Chops Italian

Everyone needs a good pork chop recipe. This one is delicious for family or when you want a special dish for company. If you are serving several people, don't double the recipe; instead make two separate casseroles. Believe me, it works better that way.

Top Of Stove
OVEN 350°

6 pork chops, ¹/₂-inch thick
1 cup uncooked long-grain rice
1 (0.7-ounce) package Italian Salad dressing mix
2¹/₂ cups boiling water
1 can Cream of Chicken soup
Salt and pepper

Trim fat from pork chops. Place fat in hot skillet to melt. Add pork chops and quickly brown over high heat. This shouldn't take more than a minute or so on each side. Meanwhile, spread rice in 13x9-inch baking dish sprayed with nonstick cooking spray. Bake in 350° oven 7-8 minutes or until light golden in color. Remove from oven. Combine dressing mix, water and soup and pour over rice. Top with pork chops. Sprinkle with salt and pepper and cover with foil. Bake at 350° for 60 minutes. Remove foil and bake 30 minutes or until liquid is absorbed. Makes 6 servings.

TIP: For 4 servings, use 4 pork chops, but use the same amount of rice and remaining ingredients.

Lighter Version:
"Healthy Request" soup

	Cal	Pro	Carb	Fib	Fat	Sat	Chol	Sod
Regular	253	16g	31g	1g	7g	2g	39mg	525mg
Lighter	239	15g	31g	1g	5g	2g	39mg	326mg

Pork Chops and Baked Bean Casserole

A nice blend of flavors.

4 loin-cut pork chops, 1/2-inch thick (about 11/2 pounds)
2 (16-ounce) cans brick oven baked beans
1/2 cup finely chopped onion
1/2 cup firmly packed light brown sugar
1/2 cup ketchup
2 teaspoons prepared mustard

Trim fat from pork chops; place fat in skillet and heat to melt. Increase heat, add pork chops and brown both sides. You want to brown the meat but you don't want the pork chops to cook through. Combine remaining ingredients and pour into an 8x8-inch baking dish sprayed with nonstick cooking spray. Arrange pork chops on top. Cover with foil and bake at 350° for 30 minutes. Remove foil and bake 30 minutes. Makes 4 servings.

TIP: Beans will be quite juicy when removed from oven, but will thicken somewhat when allowed to stand a few minutes.

	Cal	Pro	Carb	Fib	Fat	Sat	Chol	Sod
Regular	498	38g	74g	12g	9g	3g	75mg	1358mg

Sausage and Egg Casserole

A delicious spicy egg dish with a chewy cheese topping. Serve as a break-
fast, brunch or casual dinner meal. I suggest you not serve this recipe to
someone who doesn't like mushrooms. They tend to stick to the cheese and
are difficult to eat around (I know, I tried).

Top Of Stove
Oven 400°

6 eggs
¹/₄ cup sour cream
1 (12-ounce) package sausage
4 ounces fresh mushrooms, sliced
1 (4-ounce) can diced green chilies
16 ounces Mozzarella cheese, shredded

Combine eggs and sour cream until blended. Pour into 13x9-inch baking
dish sprayed with nonstick cooking spray. Bake at 400° for 10 to 12 minutes
or until eggs are set, but not too firm (they may puff up somewhat and then
fall). Meanwhile, cook sausage in skillet; drain off fat. Add mushrooms and
chilies and cook until mushrooms are tender, 2 to 3 minutes. Spoon mixture
over eggs. Sprinkle with cheese. Bake at 400° for 10 to 15 minutes or until
golden. Makes 6 to 8 servings.

VARIATIONS: Serve topped with salsa
Omit green chilies; use Monterey Jack cheese with jalapenos
Use half Cheddar and half Monterey Jack Cheese

Lighter Version:
Egg substitute
8 ounces light turkey sausage
12 ounces light Mozzarella cheese

	Cal	Pro	Carb	Fib	Fat	Sat	Chol	Sod
Regular	422	34g	6g	1g	29g	15g	281mg	1062mg
Lighter	291	30g	5g	1g	17g	10g	56mg	897mg

Rice Casserole with Sausage

A simple yet delicious family-type casserole.

1 (12-ounce) package mild sausage
1¹/₂ cups uncooked long-grain rice
1 (20-ounce) package frozen broccoli pieces
2 cans Cream of Chicken soup
¹/₂ cup milk
2 cups (8-ounces) Swiss cheese, shredded

Brown sausage and drain. Meanwhile, cook rice following package directions, but omit butter and salt. Place broccoli in a colander and rinse with hot water; drain thoroughly. Place in 13x9-inch baking dish sprayed with nonstick cooking spray. Spread rice evenly over broccoli. Combine soup, milk and ¹/₃ of the cheese. Pour over rice. Sprinkle with remaining cheese. Bake at 350° for 35 to 40 minutes or until golden. Makes 8 servings.

TIP: Make sure baking dish is at least two inches deep.

VARIATIONS: Use 2 cups cooked cubed chicken, Cream of Chicken soup and Mozzarella cheese, or chicken, Cream of Mushroom soup and Monterey Jack cheese with jalapeno peppers.

Lighter Version:
Light turkey sausage
"Healthy Request" soup
Nonfat milk
Lowfat Swiss cheese

	Cal	Pro	Carb	Fib	Fat	Sat	Chol	Sod
Regular	424	20g	41g	3g	18g	9g	51mg	979mg
Lighter	323	22g	43g	3g	7g	4g	39mg	697mg

Pasta Casserole with Mozzarella

A great tasting casserole dish that can be on your table in less than an hour.

Top Of Stove
Oven 350°

6 ounces Trio noodles (a combination of rotini-mostaccioli- small shells)
1 (12-ounce) package sausage
4 ounces fresh mushrooms, sliced
2¹/₂ cups chunky style spaghetti sauce
1 cup (4-ounces) Mozzarella cheese, shredded

Cook noodles according to package directions. Meanwhile, brown sausage in large skillet. Add mushrooms toward end of cooking time and cook briefly (they don't have to cook through). Add spaghetti sauce. Bring to a boil; reduce heat and simmer about 8 to 10 minutes. Drain noodles and add to sauce. Pour into a 1¹/₂-quart deep casserole dish sprayed with nonstick cooking spray. Sprinkle with cheese. Bake at 350° for 15 to 20 minutes or until golden. Makes 4 servings.

TIP: I am aware of one company that packages the noodles in a 12-ounce package. If they can't be found in your supermarket, substitute any combination of noodles desired. (Rotini or mostaccioli work best.)

Lighter Version:
Light turkey sausage
Light Mozzarella cheese

	Cal	Pro	Carb	Fib	Fat	Sat	Chol	Sod
Regular	531	25g	53g	5g	25g	9g	51mg	1534mg
Lighter	488	31g	52g	5g	18g	8g	61mg	1567mg

Sausage and Wild Rice Casserole

A nice, rather spicy family dish. If desired, substitute one pound lean ground beef and season with salt and pepper.

Top Of Stove
Oven 350°

1 (12-ounce) package mild sausage
¾ cup sliced celery
1 cup chopped onion
1 (6-ounce) package long-grain and wild rice mix

Crumble sausage into a large skillet; add onion and celery and cook until sausage is brown and vegetables are soft. Meanwhile, cook the rice according to package directions. Add sausage to rice; pour into 1½-quart deep casserole dish sprayed with nonstick cooking spray. Cover; bake at 350° for 20 minutes or until heated through. Makes 4 servings.

Lighter Version:
Light turkey sausage

	Cal	Pro	Carb	Fib	Fat	Sat	Chol	Sod
Regular	349	14g	41g	2g	14g	5g	36mg	584mg
Lighter	306	19g	41g	2g	7g	4g	46mg	617mg

Pancake Sausage Casserole

This is the answer for those days when you don't have time to stand and flip pancakes. Also convenient when boating and camping.

Top Of Stove
Oven 350°

12 sausage links
1$^{1}/_{2}$ cups flour
2 teaspoons baking powder
3 tablespoons oil
2 large eggs
1 cup milk

Brown sausages until almost cooked through. Place in 11x7-inch baking dish sprayed with nonstick cooking spray. Sausages should be arranged in two rows of six each. Combine remaining ingredients, mixing well to blend. Pour batter over sausages. Bake in 350° oven for 40 to 45 minutes or until cooked through. Makes 4 to 6 servings.

TIP: Serve with maple syrup or a fruit flavored syrup. If you aren't concerned about the amount of sodium in your diet, you may wish to add about $^{1}/_{2}$ teaspoon salt to the batter.

Lighter Version:
Light turkey sausage
1 tablespoon oil
Egg substitute
Nonfat milk

	Cal	Pro	Carb	Fib	Fat	Sat	Chol	Sod
Regular	474	18g	40g	2g	26g	7g	143mg	810mg
Lighter	386	27g	40g	2g	13g	5g	55mg	1031mg

Mostaccioli Sausage Casserole

The baking time is only 10 minutes for this delicious pasta casserole.

Top Of Stove
Oven 350°
Broil

10 ounces Mostaccioli
1 (12-ounce) package mild sausage
1 (28-ounce) jar chunky spaghetti sauce with onions and mushrooms
1/2 cup freshly grated Parmesan cheese
16 ounces Mozzarella cheese, shredded

Cook pasta according to package directions; drain. Meanwhile, brown sausage in large skillet; drain off fat. Add spaghetti sauce, bring to a boil, reduce heat and simmer 10 to 15 minutes. Place pasta in a 13x9-inch baking dish sprayed with nonstick cooking spray. Pour meat sauce over top and toss to coat the pasta. Sprinkle with Parmesan cheese, then the Mozzarella. Bake at 350° for 10 minutes. Remove from oven, raise shelf and turn oven to broil. Return casserole to oven and broil 2 to 3 minutes or until the cheese is golden (watch carefully). Makes 10 servings.

Lighter Version:
Light turkey sausage
Do not bake. Instead, place cooked pasta on a large serving platter and top with the meat mixture. Sprinkle with 1/4 cup Parmesan cheese (omit the Mozzarella)

	Cal	Pro	Carb	Fib	Fat	Sat	Chol	Sod
Regular	385	23g	32g	3g	18g	8g	43mg	975mg
Lighter	229	12g	31g	3g	7g	3g	20mg	702mg

Lowfat Mexican Strata

Strata-type dishes are convenient make-ahead type recipes, but are typically very high in fat and cholesterol. This lower fat version is so good, you may be tempted to over-indulge, but be cautious and you will be able to enjoy this dish more often.

Top Of Stove
Chill
Oven 350°

1 pound light turkey sausage
1 pound loaf French, Italian or sourdough bread, cubed
1 (16-ounce) jar Thick 'n Chunky mild salsa
1 (12-ounce) package light Mozzarella cheese, shredded
1¹/₂ cups egg substitute
2 cups nonfat milk

Crumble sausage into a medium skillet. Cook until browned; drain off fat. Arrange half the bread cubes in a 13x9-inch baking dish sprayed with nonfat cooking spray. Spoon 1 cup of the salsa over bread. Top with half the sausage and half the cheese. Repeat layers. Combine egg substitute and milk. Pour over top. Cover; chill 8 hours or overnight. Remove cover; bake at 350° for 40 to 45 minutes or until light golden and liquid is absorbed. Makes 12 servings.

	Cal	Pro	Carb	Fib	Fat	Sat	Chol	Sod
Regular	281	22g	24g	1g	10g	5g	37mg	865mg

Italian Sausage Casserole

A few simple ingredients makes a tasty casserole.

Top Of Stove
Oven 350°

1 cup uncooked long-grain rice
12 ounces Italian sausage
1 cup chopped onion
1 cup (4-ounces) Mozzarella cheese, diced
2 eggs, lightly beaten
2 tablespoons finely chopped parsley

Cook rice according to package directions. Meanwhile, crumble sausage into large skillet. Add onion and cook until sausage is browned and cooked through; drain off fat. Combine rice, sausage and cheese. Pour into 11x7-inch baking dish sprayed with nonstick cooking spray. Combine eggs and parsley; spread over top. Bake at 350° for 20 minutes or until heated through. Makes 6 servings.

TIP: Not as good reheated.

Lighter Version:
Light turkey sausage
Light Mozzarella cheese
Egg substitute

	Cal	Pro	Carb	Fib	Fat	Sat	Chol	Sod
Regular	305	16g	30g	1g	13g	5g	103mg	389mg
Lighter	283	20g	30g	1g	9g	5g	41mg	535mg

Egg Noodle Sausage Casserole

Your family will enjoy this simple noodle casserole with a green or jello salad, a relish tray and hot buttered rolls.

Top Of Stove
OVEN 350°

1 (12-ounce) package egg noodles
1 pound mild sausage
1 small green pepper, finely chopped
1 (28-ounce) can diced tomatoes, with juice
5 large bay leaves
¹⁄₃ cup freshly grated Parmesan cheese

Cook noodles according to package directions; drain. Meanwhile, crumble sausage in large skillet. Add green pepper and cook until sausage is browned and cooked through; drain off fat. Stir in tomatoes, bay leaves and Parmesan cheese. Add noodles and cook until heated through. Pour into a 2-quart deep casserole dish sprayed with nonstick cooking spray. Cover; bake at 350° for 20 minutes. Makes 6 servings.

TIP: If desired, save about 2 tablespoons of the Parmesan cheese and sprinkle on top before baking. If diced tomatoes aren't available, use whole tomatoes and cut up.

Lighter Version:
Light turkey sausage

	Cal	Pro	Carb	Fib	Fat	Sat	Chol	Sod
Regular	382	18g	42g	3g	16g	6g	82mg	827mg
Lighter	344	22g	41g	3g	10g	5g	91mg	856mg

Beans and Polish Sausage

*You'll enjoy this flavorful casserole dish made with kielbasa
and baked beans.*

Oven 350°

6 ounces kielbasa, diced
1 (31-ounce) can pork and beans
1/4 cup finely chopped onion
2 tablespoons firmly packed light brown sugar
2 teaspoons Dijon mustard
1/4 cup ketchup

Combine ingredients and pour into a 1¼-quart deep casserole dish sprayed with nonstick cooking spray. Bake at 350° for 1½ hours. Makes 4 servings.

Lighter Version:
3 ounces kielbasa

	Cal	Pro	Carb	Fib	Fat	Sat	Chol	Sod
Regular	387	18g	53g	11g	14g	5g	44mg	1671mg
Lighter	321	15g	53g	11g	8g	3g	30mg	1442mg

Baked Beans and Sausage

*The addition of sausage makes this a full meal when teamed
with a salad and French Bread.*

Top Of Stove
Oven 350°

**1 (12-ounce) package mild sausage
1 (31-ounce) can pork and beans
1 large Rome or Golden Delicious apple, peeled and sliced thin
1/3 cup firmly packed light brown sugar
1 tablespoon prepared mustard
1/4 cup ketchup**

Brown sausage in medium skillet; drain off fat. Combine sausage with remaining ingredients. Place in a 2-quart deep casserole dish sprayed with nonstick cooking spray. Bake at 350° for 1 1/4 to 1 1/2 hours or until sauce has thickened and apples are tender. Makes 6 servings.

<u>Lighter Version:</u>
8 ounces light turkey sausage

	Cal	Pro	Carb	Fib	Fat	Sat	Chol	Sod
Regular	303	13g	42g	8g	11g	4g	34mg	1154mg
Lighter	254	14g	43g	8g	5g	2g	31mg	1065mg

Lasagna with Pepperoni and Cheese

Surprise your family with an easy lasagna dish made with pepperoni.

9 lasagna noodles
1 (28-ounce) jar chunky spaghetti sauce (3 cups)
8 ounces (about 2 cups) dry curd ricotta or cottage cheese
1 (12-ounce) package Mozzarella cheese, shredded
6 ounces pepperoni, thinly sliced
1/4 cup freshly grated Parmesan cheese

Cook noodles according to package directions; drain and rinse thoroughly to cool. Place 3 noodles in a 13x9-inch baking dish sprayed with nonstick cooking spray. Layer with 1/3 of the spaghetti sauce, ricotta, Mozzarella and pepperoni. Repeat to make three layers. Sprinkle with Parmesan cheese. Bake at 350° for 30 minutes. Makes 8 servings.

Lighter Version:

Lowfat ricotta or cottage cheese
8 ounces light Mozzarella cheese
4 ounces pepperoni
2 tablespoons Parmesan cheese

	Cal	Pro	Carb	Fib	Fat	Sat	Chol	Sod
Regular	0	45g	65g	5g	21g	5g	88mg	872mg
Lighter	0	45g	65g	5g	14g	5g	88mg	872mg

Crab Casserole with Broccoli

This quick and easy casserole dish can be ready to eat in less than an hour.

OVEN 350°

8 small fresh broccoli spears, cooked
1 (6$^{1}/_{2}$-ounce) can crab, drained
$^{1}/_{4}$ cup finely chopped onion
$^{1}/_{2}$ cup mayonnaise
1 teaspoon prepared mustard
$^{3}/_{4}$ cup (3-ounces) Cheddar cheese, shredded

Arrange broccoli in 8x8-inch baking dish sprayed with nonstick cooking spray. Top with crab and onion. Combine mayonnaise and mustard; spread over top. Sprinkle with cheese. Bake at 350° for 25 to 30 minutes or until heated through.

Lighter Version:
Light mayonnaise
$^{1}/_{2}$ cup (2-ounces) lowfat Cheddar cheese

	Cal	Pro	Carb	Fib	Fat	Sat	Chol	Sod
Regular	435	26g	20g	11g	31g	8g	80mg	553mg
Lighter	248	24g	24g	11g	9g	2g	51mg	422mg

Tuna Quiche Casserole

This is a perfect choice for easy entertaining for almost any meal.

Oven 425°

1 (9-inch) pie shell
2 cups (8-ounces) Swiss cheese, shredded
1/2 cup finely chopped onion
1 (6^{1}/8-ounce) can tuna, drained
2 cups Half and Half
5 eggs, lightly beaten

Place pie shell in 11x7-inch baking dish sprayed with nonstick cooking spray. Press to fit bottom of dish. Trim off excess or fold toward inside of dish and press down (cover bottom of dish only). Prick surface with a fork and bake in 425° oven for 10 minutes.

Remove from oven (reduce heat to 350°) and sprinkle with cheese. Top with onion and tuna. Combine Half and Half and eggs; pour into baking dish. Bake at 350° for 40 to 45 minutes or until knife inserted in center comes out clean. Makes 6 servings.

Lighter Version:
Lowfat cheese
Solid white tuna packed in water
Nonfat milk
Egg substitute

	Cal	Pro	Carb	Fib	Fat	Sat	Chol	Sod
Regular	506	28g	21g	1g	34g	16g	250mg	443mg
Lighter	340	29g	21g	1g	15g	4g	27mg	504mg

Coffee Baked Beans

I don't know that you can really taste the coffee, but the combination of ingredients is very good.

OVEN 350°

2 (16-ounce) cans brick oven baked beans
1 cup chopped onion
1/2 cup strong coffee
1 tablespoon apple cider vinegar
1 teaspoon dry mustard
1/3 cup firmly packed light brown sugar

In large mixing bowl, combine ingredients and pour into 2-quart deep casserole dish sprayed with nonstick cooking spray. Bake, uncovered, in 350° oven for 1 1/4 to 1 1/2 hours or until mixture has thickened. Makes 8 servings.

TIP: Cooking time may vary according to how you like your baked beans - more soupy or a little thicker.

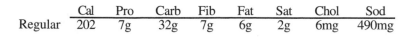

	Cal	Pro	Carb	Fib	Fat	Sat	Chol	Sod
Regular	202	7g	32g	7g	6g	2g	6mg	490mg

Sweet and Sour Baked Beans

If you haven't tried pineapple in baked beans, you must try this recipe.
Great served with hamburgers or hot dogs.

Oven 350°

1 (31-ounce) can pork and beans
1 (8-ounce) can pineapple tidbits, with juice
$1/2$ of a small green pepper, cut into narrow strips
$1/3$ cup finely chopped onion
$1/4$ cup firmly packed light brown sugar
1 tablespoon apple cider vinegar

Combine all ingredients and pour into a $1^1/2$-quart deep casserole dish sprayed with nonstick cooking spray. Bake at 350° for $1^1/2$ hours or until most of the juice has cooked down. Makes 6 servings.

	Cal	Pro	Carb	Fib	Fat	Sat	Chol	Sod
Regular	194	8g	41g	8g	2g	1g	10mg	648mg

Vegetables 199

Green Bean Casserole

In case you haven't noticed, most cans of green beans have shrunk from 16 ounces to 14.5 ounces. Now, if only the price would shrink too!

Top Of Stove
OVEN 350°

3 (14.5-ounce) cans green beans, drained
2 tablespoons melted butter
2 tablespoons flour
1 cup chopped onion
1 teaspoon salt
2 cups (8-ounces) Swiss cheese, shredded

Place green beans in a large mixing bowl. Combine melted butter and flour; add to beans. Add remaining ingredients and toss thoroughly to blend. Pour into 11x7-inch baking dish sprayed with nonstick cooking spray. Bake at 350° for 40 to 45 minutes. Makes 6 to 8 servings.

TIP: If added crunch is desired, sprinkle top lightly with sliced almonds or add 1 (5-ounce) can sliced water chestnuts, drained, to the casserole. Also good reheated.

Lighter Version:
1 tablespoon butter
Lowfat Swiss cheese

	Cal	Pro	Carb	Fib	Fat	Sat	Chol	Sod
Regular	238	14g	15g	5g	14g	9g	45mg	1028mg
Lighter	147	14g	15g	5g	4g	2g	18mg	1008mg

Broccoli Bake

*Serve for brunch or lunch with fresh fruit and delicious
hot rolls or muffins.*

Oven 375°

1 cup baking mix
1 cup milk
5 eggs, lightly beaten
1/2 cup finely chopped onion
2 cups broccoli flowerets
1 cup (4-ounces) Cheddar cheese, cubed

In large mixing bowl, combine baking mix and milk until well blended.
Stir in remaining ingredients. Pour into 8x8-inch baking dish sprayed with
nonstick cooking spray. Bake at 375° for 25 to 30 minutes or until set.
Makes 6 servings.

TIP: If the large eggs look more like small eggs, add an additional egg to the
recipe.

Lighter Version:
Nonfat milk
Egg substitute
Lowfat Cheddar cheese

	Cal	Pro	Carb	Fib	Fat	Sat	Chol	Sod
Regular	257	14g	18g	2g	14g	6g	200mg	452mg
Lighter	186	14g	18g	2g	6g	2g	5mg	373mg

Broccoli Scalloped Potatoes

This scalloped potato dish has a delightful broccoli flavor.

2 tablespoons butter
$^1/_2$ cup finely chopped onion
1 can Cream of Broccoli soup
$^1/_3$ cup milk
8 cups sliced peeled potatoes
Salt and pepper, to taste

Melt butter in small skillet; add onion and cook until soft. Remove from heat and stir in soup and milk, blending until smooth. Distribute half of the potato slices in a 11x7-inch baking dish sprayed with nonstick cooking spray. Sprinkle with salt and pepper. Top with half the soup mixture. Repeat layers. Cover with foil and bake at 350° for 60 minutes. Remove foil and bake 20 to 30 minutes or until potatoes are tender. Makes 6 servings.

VARIATION: Use Broccoli Cheese soup.

Lighter Version:
1 tablespoon butter
"Healthy Request" soup
Nonfat milk

	Cal	Pro	Carb	Fib	Fat	Sat	Chol	Sod
Regular	233	5g	41g	3g	7g	3g	17mg	475mg
Lighter	207	5g	42g	3g	3g	1g	6mg	271mg

Broccoli Dinner Casserole

A very tasty sauce served with a popular vegetable. Don't be turned off by the three methods of cooking - it is quite quick and easy.

Microwave
Top Of Stove
Oven 350°

1 large bunch fresh broccoli (about 2 pounds)
1/4 cup butter
1 cup coarsely chopped onion
1 (8-ounce) container cream cheese with herbs and garlic
1 can Cream of Mushroom soup

Cut broccoli into serving size pieces, leaving about a 2-inch stem. Place in a 13x9-inch baking dish sprayed with nonstick cooking spray. Add enough water to cover bottom (about 1/2 inch). Cover and steam in microwave about 5 minutes or just until broccoli turns a bright green. Remove and carefully pour off the hot water.

Melt butter in small skillet; add onion and cook until soft. Pour over broccoli. In small saucepan, combine soup and cream cheese. Cook, over low heat, until smooth. Pour over vegetables leaving some of the green showing. Bake at 350° for 20 minutes or until heated through. Makes 6 servings.

TIP: Make an attractive holiday dish by sauteing 1/2 red bell pepper (chopped) with the onion.

Lighter Version:
2 tablespoons butter
"Healthy Request" soup

	Cal	Pro	Carb	Fib	Fat	Sat	Chol	Sod
Regular	307	7g	17g	5g	26g	13g	62mg	665mg
Lighter	250	7g	17g	5g	19g	10g	55mg	415mg

Swiss Corn Casserole

A nice vegetable casserole to serve with most meats.

1 (15-ounce) can whole corn, drained
³/4 cup (3-ounces) Swiss cheese, shredded
¹/2 cup heavy cream
1 egg, lightly beaten
Salt and pepper, to taste

Combine ingredients; spoon into a 1-quart deep casserole dish sprayed with nonstick cooking spray. Bake at 350° for 30 minutes or until center is set. Makes 4 servings.

Lighter Version:
Lowfat Swiss cheese
Nonfat milk
Egg substitute

	Cal	Pro	Carb	Fib	Fat	Sat	Chol	Sod
Regular	287	11g	21g	2g	19g	11g	113mg	425mg
Lighter	147	12g	22g	2g	3g	1g	8mg	441mg

Sweet Potato Casserole

We tend to call both sweet potatoes and yams "sweet potatoes", but this calls for the darker orange potatoes, not the more yellow type.

Oven 450°

4 pounds yams
1 (8-ounce) can crushed pineapple, drained
¼ cup sweetened condensed milk
¼ cup firmly packed light brown sugar
½ cup chopped pecans or walnuts
15 large marshmallows

Bake potatoes in 450° oven for 60 to 70 minutes or until tender. Let cool a few minutes; carefully remove peel. Place in large mixer bowl and mash. Add next four ingredients. Pour into 8x8-inch baking dish sprayed with nonstick cooking spray. Reduce oven to 400° and bake 20 minutes or until heated through. Remove from oven and place marshmallows evenly over top. Return to oven and bake 6 to 8 minutes or until puffed and golden. Makes 8 servings.

TIP: Baking time for the potatoes will vary according to the size of the potatoes. They also tend to drip somewhat the last few minutes of baking time so you may want to cook potatoes on the top rack and place a piece of foil underneath.

Lighter Version:
¼ cup pecans or walnuts
Canned evaporated skim milk

	Cal	Pro	Carb	Fib	Fat	Sat	Chol	Sod
Regular	390	6g	81g	7g	6g	1g	3mg	43mg
Lighter	341	5g	76g	7g	3g	0g	0mg	40mg

Quick Potatoes Au Gratin

We all need recipes that are quick, inexpensive and filling. This is perfect for those busy days when you have so little time to cook. Let the kids help.

1 (12-ounce) package (or 3 cups) frozen hash brown potatoes, thawed
1 cup milk
2 tablespoons butter, melted
1 teaspoon seasoned salt
1/2 cup sliced green onions (white and green part)
11/2 cups (6-ounces) Cheddar cheese, shredded

Place thawed potatoes in 8x8-inch baking dish sprayed with nonstick cooking spray. Combine milk, butter, salt and onions; pour over top. Sprinkle with cheese. Bake at 350° for 30 minutes or until cheese is golden. Makes 4 servings.

<u>Lighter Version:</u>
Nonfat milk
1 tablespoon butter
Lowfat Cheddar cheese

	Cal	Pro	Carb	Fib	Fat	Sat	Chol	Sod
Regular	324	14g	19g	1g	21g	13g	65mg	906mg
Lighter	192	14g	19g	1g	6g	4g	18mg	622mg

Parmesan Potato Dish

You'll enjoy this flavorful potato dish made quickly with packaged hashbrowns.

Top Of Stove
Oven 350°

1 (24-ounce package) frozen hash browns (thaw about 15 to 20 minutes)
1 cup whipping cream
1/2 cup finely minced onion
1/2 cup butter, cubed
1/2 teaspoon pepper
5 tablespoons freshly grated Parmesan cheese, divided

Place hash browns and whipping cream in large saucepan. Bring mixture to a boil; reduce heat and cook until cream is absorbed, but mixture is still moist, stirring occasionally. Remove from heat; add onion, butter, pepper and 2 tablespoons of the Parmesan cheese. Stir mixture until blended. Pour into 8x8-inch baking dish sprayed with nonstick cook spray; sprinkle with remaining Parmesan. Bake at 350° for 50 to 60 minutes or until potatoes are tender and cheese has formed a nice golden crust. Makes 6 servings.

Lighter Version:
Half and Half
3 tablespoons butter
3 tablespoons Parmesan cheese

	Cal	Pro	Carb	Fib	Fat	Sat	Chol	Sod
Regular	549	7g	34g	3g	45g	25g	100mg	307mg
Lighter	370	6g	35g	3g	24g	12g	33mg	172mg

Baked Potatoes with Cream

A wonderfully rich potato dish. Easy too!

7 medium potatoes, about 7 cups sliced
2 cups whipping cream
Salt and Pepper
4 tablespoons freshly grated Parmesan cheese

Peel and slice potatoes less than ¹/₂-inch thick. Place half the potatoes in 13x9-inch baking dish sprayed with nonstick cooking spray. Pour half the cream over top. Sprinkle with salt, pepper and half the Parmesan cheese. Layer with remaining potatoes and repeat with the remaining cream, salt, pepper and Parmesan cheese. Bake at 450° (425° if using glass) for about 45 minutes or until golden and potatoes are tender. Makes 6 servings.

TIP: Watch closely last 15 minutes. If top is getting too brown, cover with foil. Baking time can vary somewhat according to how thick you slice the potatoes. Also, cooking time will take longer if you use a smaller, but deeper, baking dish.

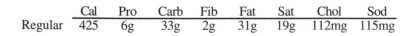

	Cal	Pro	Carb	Fib	Fat	Sat	Chol	Sod
Regular	425	6g	33g	2g	31g	19g	112mg	115mg

Baked Potato Salad with Cheese

*Since the cheese doesn't have to be refrigerated and the bacon can be cooked
at home, this makes a nice recipe for boating or camping.*

6 medium potatoes (5 cups cooked)
³/₄ pound American processed cheese, cut into ¹/₂-inch cubes
¹/₂ cup finely chopped onion
1 cup mayonnaise
Salt and pepper, to taste
¹/₂ cup cooked crumbled bacon

Cook potatoes in boiling water until just tender; let cool slightly before
peeling. Cut into small cubes. In large mixing bowl, combine potatoes with
onion and mayonnaise. Season with salt and pepper. Pour into an 8x8-inch
baking dish sprayed with nonstick cooking spray. Sprinkle bacon over top.
Bake at 350° for 30 minutes or until heated through. Makes 6 servings.

Lighter Version:
Lowfat American cheese
Light mayonnaise
Omit bacon

	Cal	Pro	Carb	Fib	Fat	Sat	Chol	Sod
Regular	646	18g	30g	2g	51g	17g	82mg	1232mg
Lighter	320	16g	37g	2g	12g	4g	30mg	1096mg

Potato Cheese Casserole

My daughter rarely salts any of her vegetables, so this recipe fits right in with her type of cooking. I prefer more salt in my potato dishes, but you be the judge for your family. This makes a very attractive company casserole.

4 pounds potatoes, peeled, boiled until tender
¹/₃ cup butter, melted
3 eggs
¹/₂ cup milk
¹/₂ cup plus 1 tablespoon freshly grated Parmesan cheese
2 cups (8-ounces) Mozzarella cheese, cubed

In large mixer bowl, mash potatoes, then add the butter, eggs, milk and ¹/₂ cup Parmesan cheese. Beat until thoroughly blended and smooth. Stir in Mozzarella cheese. Pour into 2¹/₂-quart deep casserole dish sprayed with nonstick cooking spray. Make swirls on top. Sprinkle with remaining 1 tablespoon Parmesan cheese. Bake at 375 ° for 25 to 30 minutes or until heated through and cheese is lightly browned. Makes 8 servings.

Lighter Version:
3 tablespoons butter
Egg substitute
Nonfat milk
¹/₃ cup plus 1 tablespoon Parmesan cheese
Light Mozzarella cheese

	Cal	Pro	Carb	Fib	Fat	Sat	Chol	Sod
Regular	409	17g	47g	3g	17g	10g	122mg	400mg
Lighter	359	17g	47g	3g	12g	7g	31mg	345mg

Broccoli Rice Casserole

A great way to use up any leftover rice you might have on hand.

Top Of Stove
OVEN 350°

2 cups cooked long-grain rice
2¹/₂ cups frozen broccoli stems and pieces
1 teaspoon oil
1 cup chopped onion
1 can Cream of Chicken soup
1 cup (4-ounces) Swiss cheese, shredded

Spread cooked rice evenly in 8x8-inch baking dish sprayed with nonstick cooking spray. Top with broccoli. Pour oil into small skillet. Add onion and cook over low heat until soft. Pour soup into small mixing bowl. Thin slightly by adding 2 tablespoons water. Add onion and pour over broccoli. Sprinkle with cheese. Bake at 350° 40 to 45 minutes or until cheese is golden. Makes 6 servings.

TIP: You can easily make this a main dish by adding a layer of cubed cooked chicken, turkey, ham or tuna.

Lighter Version:
"Healthy Request" soup
Lowfat Swiss cheese

	Cal	Pro	Carb	Fib	Fat	Sat	Chol	Sod
Regular	246	11g	30g	3g	9g	4g	21mg	469mg
Lighter	194	11g	31g	3g	3g	1g	11mg	269mg

Broccoli Rice with Cheese

If you like "hot", I think you will enjoy this recipe. If not, use regular Monterey Jack cheese.

Top Of Stove
Oven 350°

1 (6-ounce) box long-grain white and wild rice mix
1 large bunch fresh broccoli, about 4 cups flowerets
1 can Cream of Chicken soup
1 (5-ounce) can sliced water chestnuts, drained
1 cup (4-ounces) Monterey Jack cheese with jalapeno, shredded

Cook rice according to package directions, but omit the butter and salt. Steam broccoli until just crisp-tender. Combine rice and broccoli with remaining ingredients and place in 11x7-inch baking dish sprayed with non-stick cooking spray. Bake at 350° for 30 minutes or until heated through. Makes 6 servings.

<u>Lighter Version:</u>
"Healthy Request" soup
Lowfat Monterey Jack cheese

	Cal	Pro	Carb	Fib	Fat	Sat	Chol	Sod
Regular	260	11g	34g	3g	9g	5g	21mg	520mg
Lighter	229	12g	35g	3g	5g	3g	18mg	366mg

Rice and Onion Casserole

Very good served with grilled steaks or pork chops.

Top Of Stove
Oven 350°

6 cups onion slices (about 2-3 onions, depending on size)
3 tablespoons butter
2¹/₂ cups cooked long-grain rice
1 cup (4-ounces) Monterey Jack cheese, shredded
1 cup Half and Half
3 tablespoons freshly grated Parmesan cheese

Onions should be thinly sliced, separated into rings, and then measured. Heat butter in large skillet. Add onion and cook until tender and transparent, but do not brown. Combine onion with the rice, Monterey Jack cheese and Half and Half. Pour into 11x7-inch baking dish sprayed with nonstick cooking spray. Sprinkle with Parmesan cheese. Bake at 350° for 60 minutes or until liquid is absorbed and top is golden. Makes 6 servings.

Lighter Version:
1 tablespoon butter
Lowfat Monterey Jack cheese
Nonfat milk
1 tablespoon Parmesan cheese

	Cal	Pro	Carb	Fib	Fat	Sat	Chol	Sod
Regular	360	11g	40g	3g	17g	11g	50mg	240mg
Lighter	261	12g	40g	3g	6g	4g	20mg	212mg

Company Rice Casserole

My son Brian and his wife Addie gave this a thumbs up. It makes a wonderful side dish with chicken, pork, beef, lamb, etc.

Top Of Stove
Oven 350°

3 tablespoons butter
3 ounces Angel Hair pasta, broken into 1-inch pieces
1 cup uncooked long-grain rice
1 can French Onion soup
1 teaspoon lite soy sauce
1 (5-ounce) can sliced water chestnuts, drained, halved

Melt butter in a medium skillet. Add noodles, and stirring frequently, cook until lightly browned. Remove from heat. Stir in remaining ingredients along with 2 cups water. Pour into 1½-quart deep casserole dish sprayed with nonstick cooking spray. Bake, uncovered, at 350° for 40 to 50 minutes or until liquid is absorbed and rice is tender. Stir once during last 15 minutes of baking time. Makes 6 servings.

TIP: Recipe doubles nicely, but you will need to thoroughly stir ingredients a couple of times during baking. If stirred only once, the rice settles to the bottom and the noodles to the top. It may also be necessary to increase cooking time. Can reheat.

Lighter Version:
1 tablespoon butter

	Cal	Pro	Carb	Fib	Fat	Sat	Chol	Sod
Regular	265	6g	44g	2g	7g	4g	15mg	546mg
Lighter	231	6g	44g	2g	3g	1g	5mg	507mg

Onion Soup Rice

I don't know of anything my son Steve doesn't like (aren't I lucky) and this is one of his favorite rice dishes. It has been in our family for over thirty years and is still a favorite.

Top Of Stove
OVEN 350°

2 cups Minute Rice
1 tablespoon oil
1 (2-ounce) can mushroom stems and pieces, with juice
1 can French Onion soup
1/2 soup can water
Salt and pepper (optional)

Lightly brown rice in hot oil, but watch very carefully as the rice starts to brown. It shouldn't actually brown, but turn a light golden color. Put rice in a 1½-quart deep casserole dish sprayed with nonstick cooking spray. Add remaining ingredients and mix well. Bake, covered, at 350° for 45 to 60 minutes or until liquid is absorbed and rice is tender. Makes 6 servings.

TIP: Please do not put this recipe in a shallow baking dish unless you like your rice nice and crispy.

	Cal	Pro	Carb	Fib	Fat	Sat	Chol	Sod
Regular	142	4g	25g	1g	3g	0g	0mg	470mg

Vegetable Rice Casserole

Who said writing a cookbook isn't fun. This recipe caused me to go off my diet - way off! It can also be served as a main dish along with a nice crunchy-type salad and toasted French bread. Add your favorite dessert .

Top Of Stove
Oven 350°

1¹/₂ cups uncooked long-grain rice
1 (20-ounce) package frozen stir-fry vegetables
2 cans Cream of Mushroom soup
³/₄ cup mayonnaise
2 cups (8-ounces) Monterey Jack cheese with jalapeno, shredded

Cook rice according to package directions, but omit the butter and salt. Meanwhile, place vegetables in a colander and run under hot water to partially thaw. Place in a 13x9-inch baking dish sprayed with nonstick cooking spray. Spread cooked rice evenly over top. Combine soup and mayonnaise until blended. Stir in about ¹/₃ of the shredded cheese. Pour over rice. Sprinkle with remaining cheese. Bake at 350° for 30 to 40 minutes or until cheese is golden and starting to brown around the edges. Makes 12 servings.

TIP: This makes a very full casserole. Don't use anything any smaller than a Pyrex-type 13x9-inch baking dish 2-inches deep.

VARIATION: Substitute broccoli pieces for the vegetables.

Lighter Version:
"Healthy Request" soup
Light mayonnaise
Lowfat Monterey Jack cheese

	Cal	Pro	Carb	Fib	Fat	Sat	Chol	Sod
Regular	341	9g	30g	3g	21g	6g	25mg	608mg
Lighter	239	10g	32g	3g	8g	3g	21mg	466mg

Cheesy Rice Casserole

This makes quite a large casserole. For a smaller family, you may wish to reduce the recipe. Because of the amount of cheese used, I would suggest serving it on one of those days when you may choose not to eat meat. Add a cup of soup, a nice salad and rolls or cornbread.

OVEN 350°

$1^3/4$ **cups uncooked long-grain rice**
$1^1/3$ **cups finely chopped onion**
$1/3$ **cup butter, melted**
$1^1/2$ **cups (6-ounces) Cheddar cheese, shredded**
2 cans Consomme
$1/3$ **cup slivered almonds**

Combine all the ingredients in a large mixing bowl. Pour into a 2-quart deep casserole dish sprayed with nonstick cooking spray. Bake at 350° for $1^1/2$ hours or until all the liquid is absorbed. Makes 8 servings.

<u>Lighter Version:</u>
Omit butter
Lowfat Cheddar cheese
Substitute water chestnuts for almonds

	Cal	Pro	Carb	Fib	Fat	Sat	Chol	Sod
Regular	376	13g	40g	2g	18g	10g	43mg	599mg
Lighter	236	12g	41g	2g	2g	1g	4mg	395mg

Index

GREAT MEALS BEGIN WITH SIX INGREDIENTS OR LESS

Six Ingredients or Less Cookbook - quick and easy recipes from everyday cooking to delicious company entertaining. Sections include: Appetizers, Breads, Cookies, Desserts, Beef, Poultry, Vegetables and many more.

Six Ingredients Or Less Chicken Cookbook - dedicated to a familiar and favorite standby, from appetizers, salads and main dishes, to 20 complete menus for plan-ahead meals.

Six Ingredients Or Less Light & Healthy - great cooking your family will love, and they'll never know the recipes are good for them. Recipes include nutritional analysis for calories, fat grams, cholesterol, sodium, etc.

Six Ingredients or Less Pasta and Casserole - great pasta and casserole recipes for today's busy lifestyles. The original and lowfat version is given for each recipe.

If you cannot find our Six Ingredients or Less Cookbooks at your local store, order directly from CJ Books. Copy or fill out the order blank below and return, with your check, money order, VISA or MC number to:

SIX INGREDIENTS OR LESS
P O Box 922
GIG HARBOR, WA 98335
1-800-423-7184

Remember, Cookbooks Make Great Gifts!

Six Ingredients or Less	(_____) # of copies	$12.95 each	$_____
Six Ingredients or Less Chicken Cookbook	(_____) # of copies	$12.95 each	$_____
Six Ingredients or Less Light & Healthy	(_____) # of copies	$12.95 each	$_____
Six Ingredients or Less Pasta & Casseroles	(_____) # of copies	$14.95 each	$_____

Plus Postage & Handling (**First book $1.75, each add't book, add $1.00**) $_____
Subtotal $_____
Washington residents add 8% sales tax $_____
Total $_____

PLEASE PRINT OR TYPE
(Please double-check addition, differences will be billed)

NAME_____ PHONE (_____) _____

ADDRESS_____

CITY_____ STATE_____ ZIP_____

MC OR VISA_____ EXP_____

SIGNATURE

223